PERGAMON INTERNATIONAL LIBRARY
of Science, Technology, Engineering and Social Studies

*The 1000-volume original paperback library in aid of education,
industrial training and the enjoyment of leisure*

Publisher: Robert Maxwell, M.C.

Basic Spanish
for
Elementary Teachers

Publisher's Notice to Educators

THE PERGAMON TEXTBOOK
INSPECTION COPY SERVICE

An inspection copy of any book published in the Pergamon International Library will gladly be sent without obligation for consideration for course adoption or recommendation. Copies may be retained for a period of 60 days from receipt and returned if not suitable. When a particular title is adopted or recommended for adoption for class use and the recommendation results in a sale of 12 or more copies, the inspection copy may be retained with our compliments. If after examination the lecturer decides that the book is not suitable for adoption but would like to retain it for his personal library, then our Educators' Discount of 10% is allowed on the invoiced price. The Publishers will be pleased to receive suggestions for revised editions and new titles to be published in this important International Library.

OTHER PERGAMON TITLES OF INTEREST

BOMSE, M.D. & ALFARO, J.H.–*Practical Spanish for School Personnel, Firemen, Police-men and Community Agencies.*
BOMSE, M.D. & ALFARO, J.H.–*Practical Spanish for Medical & Hospital Personnel.*
ELLIS, A.–*How to Find Out About Children's Literature.*
ELLIS, A.–*A History of Children's Reading & Literature.*
FOSKETT, D.J.–*How to Find Out in Educational Research.*

The terms of our inspection copy service apply to all the above books. A complete catalogue of all books in the Pergamon International Library is available on request.

Basic Spanish
for
Elementary Teachers

by
Marilyn R. Seymann
Arizona State University
College of Education

PERGAMON PRESS, INC.
New York/Toronto/Oxford/Sydney/Braunschweig/Paris

Pergamon Press Offices:

U.S.A.	Pergamon Press Inc., Maxwell House, Fairview Park, Elmsford, New York 10523, U.S.A.
U.K.	Pergamon Press Ltd., Headington Hill Hall, Oxford OX3 OBW, England
CANADA	Pergamon of Canada, Ltd., 207 Queen's Quay West, Toronto 1, Canada
AUSTRALIA	Pergamon Press (Aust) Pty., Ltd., 19a Boundary Street, Rushcutters Bay, N.S.W. 2011, Australia
FRANCE	Pergamon Press SARL, 24 rue des Ecoles, 75240 Paris, Cedex 05, France
WEST GERMANY	Pergamon Press GMbH, 3300 Braunschweig, Postfach 2923, Burgplatz 1, West Germany

Copyright ©1974, 1976 Pergamon Press Inc.

Library of Congress Cataloging in Publication Data

Seymann, Marilyn R.
  Basic Spanish for elementary teachers.

  Bibliography: p.
  1. Spanish language – Grammar – 1950-
2. Elementary school teachers, Training of.
3. Education, Bilingual – United States.   I.   Title.
PC4112.S48   1975   460'.7   75-31938

ISBN 0-08-020425-2

Cover design by Nina Bookbinder
Illustrations by Cynthia Benedict

Printed in the United States of America

I would like to dedicate this book to three very special little boys: Gregory, Scott, and Jeffrey.

CONTENTS

SECTION XVI

ACKNOWLEDGEMENTS

I would like to acknowledge the assistance, interest and encouragement of two sensitive and aware individuals: each very different, each very special, each very concerned. To Dr. Henry J. Casso and Ms. Bertha Landrum--mis gracias, afecto y respeto.

To Ms. Mary McKivergan--for unselfishly sharing with me so much of yourself and for your continued support--no hay palabras.

NOTE TO INSTRUCTORS

In addition to the material provided by the text, supplementary materials in both culture and language should be employed.

Since it is essential to point out to your students the linguistic problems they may anticipate as teachers in their own classrooms, an inclusion of some comparative analysis between English and Spanish will be informative. Basic points of linguistic interference, such as "schwa" vowel sounds, intonation variances (stress, pitch, terminal junctures, rhythm, etc.), non-existent sounds in one language or the other, different sounds for the "same" letter, sh-ch reversal, air flow differences, syntactical and structural variances, "strange meanings" of lexical structures, false cognates, etc., should all be isolated, identified, and explained. It is an unfair burden to assume that each instructor be thoroughly conversant in linguistics and, therefore, I would like to recommend the use of some supplementary works which are informative and are within the grasp of the students for further reference:

Brooks, Nelson. Language and Language Learning. New York: Harcourt, Brace & World, 1960.

Bull, William E. Spanish for Teachers. New York: Ronald Press Company, 1965.

Lado, Robert. Linguistics Across Cultures. Ann Arbor: The University of Michigan Press, 1971.

Olguin, Leonard. Solutions in Communications. Acme Film & Videotape Lab, Inc., 116 North Highland Avenue, Hollywood, CA.

Stockwell, Robert P. & Bowen, J. Donald. The Sounds of English and Spanish. Chicago: The University of Chicago Press, 1965.

Additional materials for supplementary cultural awareness should be included as well. Some good biliography can be obtained in several recent publications:

Abrahams, Roger D. & Troike, Rudolph C. Language and Cultural Diversity in American Education. Englewood Cliffs, N.J.: Prentice-Hall, 1972.

Anderson, Theodore & Boyer, Mildred. Bilingual Schooling in the United States. Austin, Texas: Southwest Educational Development Laboratory, 1970.

Burger, Henry C. "Ethno-Pedagogy": A Manual in Cultural Sensitivity, With Techniques for Improving Cross-Cultural Teaching by Fitting Ethnic Patterns. Albuquerque, N.M.: Southwestern Cooperative Educational Laboratory, Inc., 1971.

Litsinger, Dolores Escobar. The Challenge of Teaching Mexican-American Students. New York: American Book Company, 1973.

From the biliographies in the aforementioned works, many incisive, sensitive studies can be obtained. It is clearly up to the discretion of the individual teacher, responding to the immediate need of the individual student, to choose the most appropriate works for reference and class discussion.

INTRODUCTION

It is rather clear that the teacher is a critical element in developing the students' academic competency and personal growth. It is also clear that to provide these students with the well prepared, sensitive teachers that they deserve, the teachers' needs must not be overlooked. To be effectively prepared to face the realities of the classroom, the teachers of Spanish-speaking students need professional training in many areas. It is the aim of this manual to meet the need in one of these areas: the Spanish language.

It is hoped that the teacher will become aware of the language through this structural approach and will be better able to function in the classroom because of an ability to speak, understand, and really hear what is being said. The aspects of the language which are covered are considered to be the most essential elements for effective, immediate communication in the language. The lexicon is a reduced one, specific to the needs of the elementary teacher. This is not intended to be a definitive linguistic work; that is not its purpose.

Since it is through the natural medium of play that the child accurately reflects feelings, experiences, values, and thoughts, this aspect of the curriculum is treated as well. The illustrative *juegos, canciones, cuentos,* and *adivinanzas* are all immediately utilizable in the classroom by the teacher because they are simple enough for both the teacher and the student to really share and enjoy. The teacher will be able to determine what may be comfortably introduced and at what point, based on the varying degrees of his own linguistic competency as well as that of the students.

This is an important consideration and one frequently overlooked by teacher trainers and material developers. It is too often assumed that the teacher is perfectly bilingual and will anticipate problems only based on the students' learning difficulties. It is important that we consider the difficulties encountered by the teachers as well.

Since communication is essential if learning is to take place, language becomes a major area of concern. While ideally a thorough knowledge of and proficiency in the language should be required, it is often an impossible goal. A basic familiarity with the language is the viable, immediate alternative.

Just as we ask the teacher to accept each student "where he is," we must make this accommodation for the teacher as well. We must maximize their abilities and provide them with the basic strengths and skills upon which they can build.

While language is seen as an essential element in communication, it is but one element. Equally important is the understanding and recognition of the inextricable bond which exists between language and culture.

Language is very much a reflection of the society which uses it. It has been suggested that a speech community might be defined not only in terms of similarities in grammar, pronunciation and vocabulary, but also in terms of a common set of values, largely unconscious, regarding the use of language in various situations. In short, language is a total system for translating meaning. Its lexical system is essentially an organization of experience.

Because cultures are reflected so vividly in the lexicon and patterns of language, learning a second language requires learning new patterns of thought and feelings as well as learning grammar and phonology.

The linguistic intolerance in our society is largely learned in schools and can be unlearned, given an informed body of teachers. An understanding of the sociolinguistic dimensions of language is, therefore, important for the teacher of minority group children, since the classroom is the place where most of our cultural attitudes toward language are passed on, either consciously or unconsciously.

The teacher must bear in mind that no language is inherently superior to any other, nor is one dialect more adequate or logical than another. A student who knows two languages or dialects may know more than the teacher and should be respected for his ability.

Switching languages or dialects (code-switching), at will, even in the middle of a sentence, is a communicative skill to be valued and not evidence of a "mixed-up language" nor a deficiency. It is a reflection of everyday speech in which the social situation determines, to a large extent, the frequency and location within the sentence where the changes from one system to another will occur. The force created by the juxtaposition of two linguistic systems is powerful poetically and psychologically.

A child with bilingual abilities should be respected for his abilities and encouraged to develop along both lines, utilizing his double linguistic and cultural potential. However, the bilingual child often presents a threat to the monolingual or bilingually insecure teacher. Since we function best under fewest insecurities and anxieties, we tend to manage our own identities by a technique of "typing" other people we observe, meet, and with whom we interact. This typing procedure is one of our major means of organizing life and making it more predictable and comfortable for us, while making it increasingly more uncomfortable for the "typed" or stereotyped. The object of this "typing" is often the minority child. The guilty party is often the teacher. Often, this stereotyping is the unconscious result of ignorance.

The less we know, the more we are subject to being involved, actively or passively, in a stereotyping situation. Stereotyping uses the cultural norms of the group doing the typing as the basis for comparison and finds the other group deficient or culturally lacking. Since it has been pointed out that stereotyping is frequently based on a lack of knowledge, you, as teachers who want to help change these situations, have the responsibility of learning as much as possible about the groups with whom you will be working. One cannot automatically control stereotyping reactions, but one can learn to control actions by learning about the different cultural systems.

By not viewing cultural differences as deprivations, by not seeking absolute correspondences across cultural boundaries, by not seeking the "natural" in human experience, we begin to understand.

It is necessary to recognize the variety of ways in which cultural differences assert themselves in various domains in our society in general and specifically in our mini sector of society--the classroom.

The classroom material will treat one of the most obvious factors of cultural difference: language. The importance of the linguistic dimension of culture cannot be overstressed. By acquiring an awareness of the structure of the language, both phonemic and syntactic, as well as of the potential points of interference and learning difficulties, you will be better equipped to listen effectively: to hear, understand, and interpret what is being said.

There are numerous other dimensions of culture which are not as obvious but are of equal importance. By acquiring a dimension of cultural awareness you can go beyond the cognitive realm of linguistic understanding: to hear what is meant by what is said. Only part of our inability to communicate is due to a lack of linguistic facility. As great a part is due to a lack of cultural awareness and sensitivity.

* * * * * *

Many of the songs, stories, poems and games used throughout the book were taken from publications of the Dissemination Center for Bilingual Bicultural Education, Austin, Texas.

The publications utilized as sources are:

1. Information and Materials to Teach the Cultural Heritage of the Mexican-American Child. November 1972. (Education Service Center, Region XIII, Austin, Texas)

2. Kindergarten Bilingual Resource Handbook. December 1972. (Lubbock Public Schools, Texas)

3. Mi Ambiente y Yo. 1973. (Corpus Christi Public Schools, Texas)

4. Resource Material for Bilingual Education. Revised edition, 1971. (Fort Worth Public Schools, Texas)

Every language (and dialect of a language) uses a limited number of classes of sounds to signal the differences between words. These distinctive sounds are called <u>phonemes</u>.

The grammatical system of the language includes all of the formal features which express meaning or the relationships of elements in sentences.

A mastery of the sound systems of both one's native tongue and that of the language of instruction, as well as an objective understanding of the unique grammar of each language is essential in bilingual classrooms where contrasting linguistic systems are being used.

Some very significant phonemic and grammatical structure differences exist between Spanish and English. We will begin by emphasizing the phonemic elements and proceed, in turn, to the grammatical elements of organization.

An additional element of importance to be noted is intonation. Intonation is a very important element in conveying meaning not carried by the words and the syntactic structure of an utterance.

Difficulties arise when the second language (L_2) does not have the same pitch levels, stress patterns, and juncture points as the first (L_1). Since we tend to transfer our entire native language system to the second language, we often project a message other than the intended one. What may appear as normal in L_1 may translate as over-insistent, or condescending in L_2, although the words are accurate.

The intonation patterns of Spanish have not been completely described. However, some basic patterns have been documented and are worth noting.

There are three ways of ending an utterance in Spanish: the pitch falls (↓); the pitch rises (↑); the pitch remains constant (|).

In the following rules, taken from William E. Bull's <u>Spanish for Teachers</u>, the numbers indicate the pitch level. Spanish has three levels of pitch (low - 1, medium - 2, high - 3). English, however, has a fourth level that is higher than any level heard in normal conversation in Spanish.

1. The uncolored statement pattern is 1211↓: *Hacemos mucho.*

2. Emphatic statements raise the last stressed syllable to pitch level three: 1231↓: *Hacemos mucho.*

3. Information questions have exactly the same patterns as statements, that is, 1211↓ for non-emphatic and 1231↓ for emphatic: *¿De dónde viene?*

4. The pattern of the yes question differs from that of the emphatic statement or emphatic information question in only one detail, the pitch remains level at the end: 1231|: *¿Estás satisfecha?*

5. The yes-no question has the pattern 1222↑: *¿Tienes tiempo?*

As we begin, try to remember that while English has many plosive sounds which require vigorous output of air, in Spanish the airflow is low and you will note the lack of certain English sounds (e.g., unvoiced th, sh, j) and the absence of many blended, neutral and slurred vowel sounds.

El Alfabeto

a	- *a*	n	- *ene*
b	- *be*	ñ	- *eñe*
c	- *c*	o	- *o*
ch	- *che*	p	- *pe*
d	- *de*	q	- *(cu)*
e	- *e*	r	- *ere*
f	- *efe*	rr	- *erre*
g	- *ge*	s	- *ese*
h	- *hache*	t	- *te*
i	- *i*	u	- *u*
j	- *jota*	v	- *uve*
l	- *ele*	x	- *equis*
ll	- *elle*	y	- *i griega*
m	- *eme*	z	- *zeta*

The Alphabet

The Spanish alphabet has the same letters as the English alphabet and four additional characters: *ch, ll, ñ,* and *rr.* Each letter has basically one sound except *c* and *g* which have two or more sounds as they do in English.

A has the <u>a</u> sound of <u>father</u>.

Examples:

animal	<u>animal</u>	*abril*	<u>April</u>
ayudar	<u>to help</u>	*agosto*	<u>August</u>
agua	<u>water</u>		
amigo	<u>friend</u>		

B has the <u>b</u> sound of <u>book</u> when it begins a breath group or a sentence and when it follows *m* or *n*. The Spanish <u>b</u> and <u>v</u> have the same sound.

Examples:

blanco	<u>white</u>	*hombre*	<u>man</u>
boca	<u>mouth</u>	*brazo*	<u>arm</u>
bañar	<u>to bathe</u>		

The sound of <u>b</u> becomes softened when it is located between vowels.

Examples:

cabeza	<u>head</u>
caballo	<u>horse</u>

C has two sounds. Before <u>e</u> and <u>i</u> it has the <u>c</u> sound of <u>city</u>.

Examples:

medicina	<u>medicine</u>	*cebra*	<u>zebra</u>
círculo	<u>circle</u>	*ciego*	<u>blind</u>
cena	<u>dinner</u>	*cielo*	<u>sky</u>

In all other cases, c has the hard c sound of cough.

Examples:

cama	bed	*cuerpo*	body
cuello	neck	*cara*	face
cosa	thing		

Ch has the ch sound of church, but not quite as strong. In the Spanish alphabet, this character immediately follows c.

Examples:

muchacho	boy	*ocho*	eight
chile	chili	*cuchara*	spoon
chica	girl	*salchicha*	sausage
chocolate	chocolate	*cuerda*	rope, string

D has the English d sound, made with the tongue against the upper front teeth, when it begins a breath group and when it follows l or n. At the end of a word, it is very quiet.

Examples:

diferente	different	*diciembre*	December
dolor	pain	*dientes*	teeth
doctor	doctor	*el día*	the day
domingo	Sunday	*usted*	you

Following other letters, d has the th sound of they.

Examples:

cuidado	care	*lado*	side
madre	mother	*padre*	father

E has two sounds in Spanish. In open syllables--when e is the final letter--e has the English long a sound of day with no diphthongal sound.

Examples:

pecho	chest	*desigual*	unequal, unlike
elote	corn (Mexican)	*edad*	age

In closed syllables--when another letter follows--it has the sound of the e in bet.

Examples:

enfermedad	sickness	*enero*	January
espalda	back	*estómago*	stomach
estornudar	to sneeze		

F has the same sound as in English.

Examples:

febrero	February	*fiesta*	party, holiday
frío	cold	*fecha*	date
frijoles	kidney beans		

G has the g sound of go before vowels a, o, and u, and before all consonants.

Examples:

gordo	fat	*gusano*	worm
gafas	glasses	*gato*	cat

Before e and i, g has the strongly aspirated h sound of house.

Examples:

gente	people	*gigante*	gigantic, giant
gis	crayon		

To retain the g sound of go before e and i, u is inserted after g. The u is silent. Gu has a w sound before o or a.

Example:

guitarra	guitar	*guante*	glove

To retain the u sound following g before e or i, place a dieresis (¨) over the u. Thus, ü.

Examples:

vergüenza	shame	*agüero*	omen, sign
		bilingüe	bilingual

H is silent in Spanish.

Examples:

humano	human	*hueso*	bone
hielo	ice	*huevo*	egg
hogar	home	*hacer*	to do, to make

I has the ee sound of knee.

Examples:

irritable	irritable	*igual*	equal
incómodo	uncomfortable	*instrumento*	instrument
invierno	winter		

J has the strongly aspirated h sound of house (or a soft gutteral sound). The English j sound, a plosive one requiring a high output of air, does not exist in Spanish.

Examples:

jueves	Thursday	*ojos*	eyes
junio	June	*orejas*	ears
julio	July	*trabajar*	to work
juego	game	*tijeras*	scissors

K occurs only in foreign words and has the foreign k sound.

L has the english l sound, made with the tongue nearly flat and the tip close to the front teeth.

Examples:

lengua	tongue	*lágrimas*	tears
lunes	Monday	*labios*	lips
libro	book		

LL is considered a single symbol. It follows l in the Spanish alphabet. The character ll has the lli sound of million or the sound of the English consonant y in yes.

Examples:

tobillos	ankles	*llover*	to rain
llorar	to cry	*tortilla*	tortilla, omelet
llamar	to call	*pollo*	chicken
amarillo	yellow		

M has the English m sound.

Examples:

morir	to die	*marzo*	March
manos	hands	*mayo*	May
martes	Tuesday	*miércoles*	Wednesday
mamá	mommy		

N has the English n sound.

Examples:

noviembre	November	*nombre*	name
número	number	*negro*	black
nacer	to be born	*nariz*	nose

Ñ occurs after n in the Spanish alphabet. It has the ny sound of canyon.

Examples:

año	year	*niño*	boy
puño	fist	*sueño*	sleep

O has the o sound of obey in open syllables ending with o.

Examples:

otoño	Autumn	*ojo*	eye
orinar	to urinate	*oreja*	ear
oso	bear		

In closed syllables--when another letter follows o--o has the o sound of order.

Examples:

señor	Mr., sir	*con*	with
octubre	October	*objeto*	object, purpose

P has the English p sound, but without the puff of breath that often accompanies this sound in English.

Examples:

pájaro	bird	*primavera*	Spring
pecho	chest	*pierna*	leg
pie	foot	*piel*	skin
paz	peace		

Q has the English k sound. Ue or ui always follows q and the u is silent.

Examples:

izquierdo	left	*pequeño*	small
quejar	to complain	*bloque*	block
tranquilo	tranquil		

R has a slightly trilled sound.

Examples:

pariente	relative	*puerco-espín*	porcupine
pero	but	*estar*	to be
puerco	pig		

When r begins a word, and after l, n, and s, it is strongly trilled.

Examples:

resfriado	cold	*rojo*	red
rodillas	knees	*rectángulo*	rectangle
ropa	clothes	*redondo*	round

RR has a forcibly trilled sound. In the Spanish alphabet it occurs after r.

Examples:

arroz	rice	*perro*	dog
arreglar	to arrange	*pizarrón*	blackboard (N.M.)
pizarra	blackboard		

S has the hissing s sound of sister.

Examples:

sangre	blood	*sábado*	Saturday
sol	sun	*septiembre*	September
silla	chair		

T has the English t sound.

Examples:

toser	to cough	*taco*	taco
tragar	to swallow	*tierra*	land
triángulo	triangle		

U has the oo sound of moon.

Examples:

último	last	*usar*	to use
uno	one	*único*	only

V has the English <u>b</u> sound.

Examples:

viernes	<u>Friday</u>	*verano*	<u>summer</u>
vestirse	<u>to dress</u>	*vecino*	<u>neighbor</u>
vaquero	<u>cowboy</u>		

The sound of <u>v</u> is softened when <u>v</u> is located between vowels.

Examples:

vivir	<u>to live</u>	*la voz*	<u>voice</u>

W occurs only in foreign words and has the foreign <u>w</u> sound.

X has the English <u>gs</u> sound when it occurs between vowels.

Examples:

examen	<u>examination</u>	*exacto*	<u>exact</u>, <u>accurate</u>
exigir	<u>to demand</u>, <u>to require</u>		

<u>X</u> has the English <u>s</u> sound before consonants. Some people pronounce the Spanish <u>x</u> before a consonant as in English.

Examples:

explicar	<u>to explain</u>	*excusado*	<u>toilet</u>
extranjero	<u>alien</u>		

Y is a consonant only when it begins a word or syllable. As a consonant it has the <u>y</u> sound of <u>yes</u>.

Examples:

yerba	<u>grass</u> (Cuban)	*payaso*	<u>clown</u>
ya	<u>already</u>	*yo*	<u>I</u>

Standing alone, <u>y</u> means <u>and</u> and has the English long <u>e</u> sound.

Z has the same sound value as <u>c</u> has before <u>e</u> or <u>i</u>--that is, the soft sound of <u>see</u>.

Examples:

zumbido	<u>buzzing</u>	*brazo*	<u>arm</u>
zapato	<u>shoe</u>	*zurdo*	<u>left-handed</u>

However, the letter z rarely appears before e or i in Spanish. In conjugating verbs and in pluralizing nouns ending in z, change to c before e. There is no conjugation where the letter i follows z.

Examples:

comenzar	to begin	*comencé*	I began
nariz	nose	*narices*	noses

Vowels

In Spanish, the five vowels are very important; their sounds are full and clear, compared to the consonants which often have obscure or even suppressed sounds. Unlike English, each vowel has only one basic sound, with slight variations according to its placement within the word. To review, vowels have the following sounds:

a like a in ah
e like a in hay
i like ee in bee
o like o in hope
u like oo in room
y (when a vowel) like the e in eat

Vowels always retain the same sounds, although they are somewhat fainter when not stressed. They gradually descend in strength as follows: a, o, e, i, and u. Traditionally, we call a, o, and e strong vowels, and i and u weak vowels.

Diphthongs

Spanish vowels do not change their basic sound when they form part of a diphthong. They are merely pronounced more rapidly in succession and form one syllable. To form diphthongs, combine a weak plus a strong vowel, a strong plus a weak vowel, or two weak vowels in one syllable. Strong vowels are a, e, and o; weak vowels are i, u, and y. Two strong vowels cannot occur in the same syllable. To retain the weak vowel's full value when it appears combined with a strong vowel, write an accent mark over the weak vowel. This forms two syllables and breaks up the diphthong.

Ai or ay has the y sound of rye.

Examples:

aire	air	*maíz*	corn
hay	there is, there are	*traigo*	I bring
		bailar	to dance

Ei or ey has the ey sound of they.

Examples:

ley	law	*seis*	six
veinte	twenty	*reír*	to laugh

Oi or oy has the oy sound of boy.

Examples:

doy	I give	*voy*	I am going
oigo	I hear	*soy*	I am
hoy	today	*estoy*	I am

Au has the ow sound of cow.

Examples:

aula	classroom	*jaula*	cage
aunque	although	*causa*	cause

Eu has the eu sound of Europe.

Examples:

deuda	debt, fault	*farmacéutico*	pharmacist

In the following groups, u and i precede other vowels. Consider them semiconsonants: u plus a vowel sounds like an English w; i plus a vowel sounds like an English y.

Ua

Examples:

cuanto	how much	*cuando*	when
cuatro	four	*lengua*	tongue
igual	equal, even		

Ue

Examples:

puerta	door	*bueno*	good
huevo	egg	*cuento*	story
abuelo	grandfather		

Uo

Example:

cuociente	quotient

Ui

Examples:

cuidado	care	*ruido*	noise
construir	to build		

Ia

Examples:

hacia	toward	*farmacia*	pharmacy
viajar	to travel	*alegría*	happiness, joy

Ie

Examples:

nadie	no one	*nieve*	snow, ice cream
tiempo	time (length)	*viejo*	old
merienda	snack		

Io

Examples:

adiós	goodbye	*río*	river
atención	attention	*indio*	Indian
mediodía	noon		

Iu

Examples:

ciudad	city	*ciudadano*	citizen

Stress the strong vowel of these diphthongs in a stressed syllable. Stress the second vowel of a diphthong formed by two weak vowels in a stressed syllable.

Following q or g, ue and ui are not diphthongs; the u is silent.

Dividing Syllables

When dividing words into syllables, the fundamental rule is to make each syllable end in a vowel and join a consonant occurring between vowels to the following vowel.

Examples:

a-mi-go	friend	*e-ne-ro*	January
ma-ña-na	tomorrow		

Separate two strong vowels.

Examples:

le-o	I read	*ca-er*	to fall
le-e	he reads		

Usually, separate two consonants between vowels.

Examples:

cin-co	five	*pron-to*	soon
her-ma-no	brother	*par-te*	part

If more than two consonants occur between vowels, join the final consonant to the second vowel.

Examples:

cons-tan-te	constant	*ins-tan-te*	instant

A prefix is a separate syllable.

Examples:

ex-pre-sar	to express	*con-se-guir*	to obtain

Consider ch, ll, and rr to be one letter and never separate them.

Examples:

mu-cha-cho	boy	*ca-lle*	street
ser-vi-lle-ta	napkin	*cu-chi-llo*	knife
pe-rro	dog		

Do not separate a consonant followed by r or l, except rl, sl, tl, sr, and nr.

Examples:

ha-blar	to speak	*li-bre*	free
en-trar	to enter	*hom-bre*	man
pro-ble-ma	problem		

but

is-la	island	*tras-la-dar*	to move
char-la	chat		

Do not separate the vowels of a diphthong or triphthong.

Examples:

jui-cio	judgment	*puer-ta*	door
hue-so	bone	*true-no*	thunder

Accentuation

In Spanish, as in English, we pronounce some syllables more forcibly than others. We call this forcible utterance stress and indicate it with an accent mark (´).

As it would be laborious to write an accent mark over every word, and as words with similar endings are generally stressed alike, words have been grouped into classes and generally do not need an accent mark. Only words that are exceptional require an accent mark.

In the following lists, we have indicated the syllables and under-lined the stressed syllable.

Stress the next to the last syllable of words ending in n, s, or a vowel.

Examples:

mer-ca-do	market	*ju-gue-te*	toy
or-den	order	*u-no*	one, a
ban-de-ra	flag	*man-za-na*	apple
me-sa	table		

Stress the last syllable of words ending in a consonant other than n or s.

Examples:

mu-jer	women	*us-ted*	you
ca-lor	heat	*pre-gun-tar*	to ask a question
com-prar	to buy	*ma-yor*	greater, older

Words stressed contrary to the two foregoing rules bear the written accent over the <u>vowel</u> of the stressed syllable.

Examples:

<u>lá</u>-piz	pencil	di-<u>fí</u>-cil	difficult
lec-<u>ción</u>	lesson	<u>plá</u>-ta-no	banana
<u>fá</u>-cil	easy	co-ra-<u>zón</u>	heart
jar-<u>dín</u>	garden	ma-te-<u>má</u>-ti-cas	math

Certain words bear an accent mark to distinguish them from words otherwise spelled alike and pronounced alike that have a different meaning. This accent mark is called diacritic.

Examples:

sí	<u>yes</u>	dé	<u>give</u>
si	<u>if</u>	de	<u>of, from</u>
él	<u>he</u>	mí	<u>me</u>
el	<u>the</u>	mi	<u>my</u>
tú	<u>you</u>	té	<u>tea</u>
tu	<u>your</u>	te	<u>you</u>

Use an accent mark to distinguish interrogative and exclamatory words from pronouns and adverbs.

Examples:

¿cuánto?	<u>how much?</u>	¿cómo?	<u>how?</u>
cuanto	<u>how much</u>	como	<u>like</u>
¿cuándo?	<u>when?</u>	¿quién?	<u>who?</u>
cuando	<u>when</u>	quien	<u>who</u>
¿dónde?	<u>where?</u>	¿qué?	<u>what?</u>
donde	<u>where</u>	que	<u>what</u>

An accent mark over the weak vowel separates a weak vowel and a strong vowel, or a strong vowel and a weak vowel and forms two syllables.

Place an accent mark over the accented weak vowel of a diphthong or tripthong and over the first of two weak vowels.

Examples:

dí-a	<u>day</u>	le-í-do	<u>read</u>
san-dí-a	<u>watermelon</u>	pa-ís	<u>country</u>

Práctica

Vamos a practicar los nombres.

¿Cómo te llamas? (What is your name?)
Hola. Me llamo . . . (My name is . . .)

Alberto	Herberto	Adela	Francisca (Paquita)
Agustín	Horacio	Aida	Gertrudis
Alejandro	Isidro, Isidoro	Alicia	Gloria
Alfonso	Jaime	Amada	Gracia
Alfredo	Javier	Ana	Inés
Álvaro	Jesús	Anita	Irene
Andrés	Joaquín	Antonia	Isabel
Ángel	Jorge	Bárbara	Josefa (Pepita),
Antonio	José (Pepe)	Benigna	Josefina
Arturo	Juan	Blanca	Juana, Juanita
Benito	Luis	Carlota	Leonor
Benjamín	Manuel	Carmen	Lucía
Carlos	Mariano	Carolina	Luisa
Diego	Miguel	Caterina	Magdalena
Domingo	Pablo	Catalina	Manuela
Eduardo	Pedro	Clara	Margarita
Enrique	Rafael	Concha	María, Mariana,
Esteban	Ramón	Consuelo	Marisela
Eugenio	Raúl	Cristina	Marta
Federico	Ricardo	Dina	Nilda
Felipe	Roberto	Dolores	Raquel
Francisco (Paco,	Rodrigo	Dorotea	Rosa
Pancho)	Salvador	Elena	Rosaria
Gerardo	Samuel	Eloísa	Rosalía
Germán	Teodoro	Elvira	Rosalinda
Guillermo	Tomás	Enriqueta	Rufina
Gustavo	Vicente	Esperanza	Sara
Héctor	Victor	Felicidad	Sofía
		Felipa	Susana
			Teresa

OBJECTIVE: Develop correct pronunciation of students' names.

REPASO

I. *¿Cómo te llamas?*

    Vamos a pronunciar los nombres de los niños de la clase.

II. *¿Cómo se dice en español?*

head	_____	bird	_____
horse	_____	small	_____
friend	_____	block	_____
man	_____	round	_____
spoon	_____	blackboard	_____
corn	_____	sun	_____
party	_____	triangle	_____
fat	_____	to live	_____
crayon	_____	shoe	_____
Monday	_____	grandfather	_____
eyes	_____	good	_____
book	_____	classroom	_____
hands	_____	goodbye	_____
land	_____	city	_____
clothes	_____	to speak	_____

III. It is a truism of linguistic studies that an accurate contrastive analysis between the language of the learner and the target language will facilitate the recognition of likely areas of difficulty.

With your new awareness of the sound system of Spanish and its comparative features with English, identify possible points of interference which could be anticipated in a Spanish-speaking child learning English. By example and explanation, how would you work with the child to eliminate these difficulties and install correct English sounds without undermining the native language?

IV. *¿Cómo se dividen en sílabas las palabras?*

padre	_____	rojo	_____
domingo	_____	pronto	_____
tortilla	_____	calle	_____
manzana	_____	ayudar	_____
bandera	_____	primavera	_____
juguete	_____	oso	_____
niño	_____	llamar	_____
negro	_____		

V. *Indique Vd donde cae el acento de la voz.*

VI. *Poemas*. *Vamos a practicarlos en voz alta.*

Rima para escoger

Pin marín
de don Pingüé
cúcara, mácara
Pípiri fue.

Los días de la semana

Lunes, martes, miércoles, - tres
Jueves, viernes, sábado, - seis
y domingo - siete

Tortillitas

Tortillitas, tortillitas,
tortillitas para papá,
tortillitas de harina
para papá cuando está enojado;
tortillitas de manteca
para mamá que está contenta.

VII. *Canciones*

Buenos días

Buenos días, a ti
Buenos días, a ti
Buenos días amigo _____
Buenos días a ti.

Diez inditos

Uno, dos y tres inditos,
cuatro, cinco, seis inditos,
siete, ocho, nueve inditos,
diez inditos chiquitos.

The Present Indicative Tense of Regular Verbs

In Spanish, verbs are conjugated to show mood, tense, person, and number. Most verb conjugations follow a regular pattern. Verbs that do not follow the pattern are irregular and you must memorize them. Even these irregular verbs are not irregular in all tenses.

Use the infinitive to form all conjugations and tenses. Verbs with the infinitive ending in -ar are first conjugation verbs, those with an -er ending are second conjugation verbs, and those with an -ir ending are third conjugation verbs.

To form the present indicative tense, obtain the stem or radical by dropping the infinitive ending, -ar, -er, or -ir. Then, attach the proper endings (shown below) for first, second, and third conjugation verbs. The English words characterizing the present indicative tense are do, does, am, are, and is plus the meaning of the verb.

First Conjugation Verbs

To form the present indicative tense of regular verbs ending in -ar, drop -ar and attach the following endings: -o, -as, -a, -amos, -áis, and -an. As an example, we have conjugated *ayudar* (to help):

yo ayud-o = ayudo	I help, I do help, I am helping
tú ayud-as = ayudas	You (familiar singular) help, do help, are helping
él ayud-a = ayuda	He helps, does help, is helping
ella ayud-a = ayuda	She helps, does help, is helping
usted ayud-a = ayuda	You (polite, singular) help, do help, are helping
nosotros ayud-amos = ayudamos	We help, we do help, we are helping
vosotros ayud-áis = ayudáis	You (familiar plural) help, do help, are helping
ellos ayud-an = ayudan	They help, do help, are helping
ellas ayud-an = ayudan	They (feminine) help, do help, are helping
ustedes ayud-an = ayudan	You (polite plural) help, do help, are helping

Second Conjugation Verbs

To conjugate the present indicative tense of verbs ending in -er, drop -er and attach the following endings: -o, -es, -e, -emos, -éis, and -en. We have conjugated *comprender* (to understand):

yo comprend-o = comprendo	nosotros comprend-emos = comprendemos
tú comprend-es = comprendes	vosotros comprend-éis = comprendéis
él comprend-e = comprende	ellos comprend-en = comprenden
ella comprend-e = comprende	ellas comprend-en = comprenden
Ud. comprend-e = comprende	Uds. comprend-en = comprenden

To translate the conjugation of *comprender*, follow the translation of *ayudar*.

Third Conjugation Verbs

To conjugate the present indicative tense of verbs ending in -ir, drop -ir and attach the following endings: -o, -es, -e, -imos, -ís, and -en. We have conjugated *escribir* (to write):

yo escrib-o = escribo	nosotros escrib-imos = escribimos
tú escrib-es = escribes	vosotros escrib-ís = escribís
él escrib-e = escribe	ellos escrib-en = escriben
ella escrib-e = escribe	ellas escrib-en = escriben
Ud. escrib-e = escribe	Uds. escrib-en = escriben

Again, to translate the conjugation of *escribir*, follow the translation of *ayudar*.

Personal Pronouns

The personal pronouns are:

yo	I
tú	You (familiar singular)
él, ella, usted (Vd.)	He, she, you (polite singular)
nosotros	We
vosotros	You (familiar plural)
ellos, ellas, ustedes (Vds.)	They (masculine), they (feminine), you (polite plural)

Although in English pronouns are always used as subjects of verbs, in Spanish we usually omit personal pronouns as subjects of verbs and use them only to clarify or emphasize.

Forming Questions and Negative Statements

To form a question, invert the subject and the verb.

Examples:

Ella escribe.	She writes. She is writing. (statement)
¿Escribe ella?	Does she write? Is she writing? (question)
Ellos comprenden.	They understand. (statement)
¿Comprenden ellos?	Do they understand? (question)
Nosotros ayudamos.	We help. (statement)
¿Ayudamos nosotros?	Are we helping? (question)

To form a negative statement or question, place the word _no_ immediately before the verb.

Examples:

Ella ayuda.	She helps. (affirmative statement)
Ella no ayuda.	She doesn't help. (negative statement)
Ellos escriben.	They are writing. (affirmative statement)
Ellos no escriben.	They are not writing. (negative statement)
¿Comprendes tú?	Do you understand? (affirmative question)
¿No comprendes tú?	Don't you understand? (negative question)

The last example illustrates how to form a negative question. The subject pronoun follows the verb and _no_ directly precedes the verb.

SOME REGULAR VERBS

First Conjugation Verbs (-ar Endings)

acabar	- to finish	*acompañar*	- to accompany
aconsejar	- to advise	*adivinar*	- to guess
alimentar	- to feed, to nourish	*amar*	- to love
		atar	- to tie, to attach
arreglar	- to arrange	*ayudar*	- to help
bailar	- to dance	*bajar*	- to descend
borrar	- to erase	*brillar*	- to shine
buscar	- to look for	*callar*	- to silence, to be silent
cambiar	- to change		
cantar	- to sing	*cepillar*	- to brush
clasificar	- to classify, to arrange	*colorear*	- to color
		comparar	- to compare
completar	- to complete, to finish	*comprar*	- to buy
		constar de	- to consist (of or in)
cortar	- to cut	*cruzar*	- to cross
dejar	- to leave, cease	*desayunar*	- to eat breakfast
desarollar	- to develop	*descansar*	- to rest
desear	- to want	*dibujar*	- to draw
dudar	- to doubt	*emplear*	- to use, to employ
entrar	- to enter	*enseñar*	- to teach
escuchar	- to listen (to)	*esperar*	- to wait (for)
estudiar	- to study	*formar*	- to form
funcionar	- to function	*ganar*	- to earn, to win
gastar	- to spend, to use up	*gozar*	- to enjoy
		hablar	- to speak
hallar	- to find	*imaginar*	- to imagine
inventar	- to invent	*levantarse*	- to get up
llamar(se)	- to call, to be called	*llegar*	- to arrive
		llevar	- to carry, to wear
llorar	- to cry	*mandar*	- to command, to order
mejorar	- to improve	*mezclar*	- to mix
mirar	- to look at	*multiplicar*	- to multiply
necesitar	- to need	*olvidar*	- to forget
ordenar	- to arrange, to order	*pasar*	- to pass, to spend time
		pasar lista	- to take roll
pintar	- to paint	*platicar*	- to chat
preguntar	- to ask, to question	*preparar*	- to prepare
		pronunciar	- to pronounce
quitar	- to remove, take away, take off	*restar*	- to subtract
		sacar	- to take out
señalar	- to show, to indicate	*separar*	- to separate
		significar	- to mean
sumar	- to add	*terminar*	- to end, to finish
tocar	- to touch	*tomar*	- to drink, to take
trabajar	- to work	*usar*	- to use
viajar	- to travel		

Second Conjugation Verbs (-er Endings)

aprender	- to learn
beber	- to drink
comer	- to eat
comprender	- to understand
correr	- to run
deber	- to owe, ought, should, must
esconder	- to hide
meter	- to put in
responder	- to respond, to answer
suceder	- to happen, to turn out
temer	- to fear

Third Conjugation Verbs (-ir Endings)

abrir	- to open
añadir	- to add
cubrir	- to cover
decidir	- to decide
escribir	- to write
permitir	- to permit
recibir	- to receive
subir	- to go up, to climb up
unir	- to connect, to unite, to join
vivir	- to live

REPASO

I. *¿Cómo se dice en español?*

1. The child cuts the paper. _____

2. Where do you live? _____

3. The teacher is using the chalk. _____

4. She is writing on the blackboard. _____

5. Are you (*tú*) drawing a circle, Juanito? _____

   _____

6. No, I am coloring a clown. _____

7. Are you (all) working hard? _____

8. What are you eating? _____

9. Juanito opens the book and looks at the pictures. _____

_____

10. María erases the board and helps in the class. _____

_____

11. We are singing *"Buenos días"* and we are learning the words. _____

_____

12. We run to (the) school and study the lesson. _____

_____

13. They are completing the set. _____

14. Juanito and Rosa are mixing the paints and they don't need help.

_____

15. We subtract five from ten. _____

16. The children wash the dog. _____

17. The teacher listens and watches the game. _____

_____

18. The class looks at the six blocks. _____

19. We sing "The Days of the Week." _____

20. The circles represent numbers and we add the numbers. _____

_____

21. The children are listening to the story of "The Three Bears." _____

_____

22. The sun shines in the sky and the birds live in a nest in the tree.

_____

23. We buy the flour in a store and my mother prepares tortillas at home.

_____

24. The fish swim in the water and don't eat much. _____

_____

25. The body works when we walk, study and eat. _____

_____

26. Luis cuts out the shapes and pastes the shapes on the paper. _____

_____

27. The children form a circle and cover their (the) eyes. _____

_____

28. They dance in a circle and listen to the music. _____

_____

29. What are you wearing today, Isabel? _____

_____

30. The children are crying because they don't understand. _____

_____

II. *Práctica de verbos*

   ¿Puede usted conjugar los verbos siguientes en las personas indicadas?

   Yo (necesitar) _____   *El* _____

   Ellos (aprender) _____   *Yo* _____

   Nosotros (abrir) _____   *Tú* _____

   Ella (esconder) _____   *Yo* _____

   Usted (hallar) _____   *Ellos* _____

   El (comer) _____   *Ustedes* _____

   Ellas (llorar) _____   *Nosotros* _____

   Tú (hablar) _____   *Yo* _____

   Ustedes (vivir) _____   *Usted* _____

   Yo (usar) _____   *El* _____

III. *Canción*

De Esta Manera Lavamos La Ropa

(This is the Way We Wash Our Clothes)

De esta manera lavamos la ropa,
lavamos la ropa, lavamos la ropa,
De esta manera lavamos la ropa, el
lunes por la mañana.

De esta manera planchamos la ropa,
planchamos la ropa, planchamos la ropa,
De esta manera planchamos la ropa,
el martes por la mañana.

De esta manera limpiamos el piso,
lipiamos el piso, limpiamos el piso,
De esta manera limpiamos el piso
el miércoles por la mañana.

De esta manera cosemos la ropa,
cosemos la ropa, cosemos la ropa,
De esta manera cosemos la ropa,
el jueves por la mañana.

De esta manera limpiamos la casa,
limpiamos la casa, limpiamos la casa,
De esta manera limpiamos la casa, el
viernes por la mañana.

De esta manera cocemos el pan,
cocemos el pan, cocemos el pan,
De esta manera cocemos el pan, el
sábado por la mañana.

De esta manera nos vamos a misa,
nos vamos misa, nos vamos a misa,
De esta manera nos vamos a misa, el
domingo por la mañana.

IV. *Adivinanzas*

La lluvia

¿Qué anuncian los truenos,
relámpagos y rayos?

La cuchara

Con ella comes la sopa,
el helado, la jalea
y otras muchísimas cosas.

El pato

Muy contento y gracioso
en el agua nada,
mientras canta,
cua-cua-cuá, cua-cua-cuá.

El teléfono

Levanto la bocina,
luego marco el número
y una voz contesta,
prontito, en seguida.

V. *Juegos*

a) *¿Qué deseas?*

Deseo un burro
No deseo un burro
¿Qué deseas tú, Juanito?

b) *¿Qué buscas?*
Busco un dulce

c) *Cambio de verbos*

Un muchacho <u>contesta</u>
Dos muchachos <u>contestan</u>

Un perro <u>ladra</u>
Dos perros <u>ladran</u>

Although the verbs *ser* and *estar* both mean <u>to be</u>, they cannot be used interchangeably without altering the meaning of the sentence. Both *ser* and *estar* are irregular in the present indicative tense.

Using *Ser*

The conjugation of the present indicative tense of *ser* is as follows:

yo soy	<u>I am</u>	*nosotros somos*	<u>We are</u>
tú eres	<u>You are</u>	*vosotros sois*	<u>You are</u> (fam. pl.)
él es	<u>He is</u>	*ellos son*	<u>They are</u>
ella es	<u>She is</u>	*ellas son*	<u>They are</u>
usted es	<u>You are</u>	*ustedes son*	<u>You are</u> (pl.)

Ser mainly expresses what is essential or characteristic of a person or thing. It denotes generally who or what a person or thing is. It expresses such conditions as:

<u>Age</u>:

El alumno es joven.   <u>The pupil is young.</u>

<u>Character</u>:

Ella es una mujer buena.   <u>She is a good woman.</u>

<u>Financial Status</u>:

El es rico.   <u>He is rich.</u>

<u>Appearance</u>:

María es muy bonita.   <u>Maria is very pretty.</u>

<u>Origin</u>:

Yo soy de Méjico.   <u>I am from Mexico.</u>

<u>Ownership</u>:

El libro es de Pedro.   <u>The book is Pedro's.</u>

<u>Material (of which a thing is made)</u>:

El bloque es de madera.   <u>The block is made of wood.</u>

Occupation:

Roberto es cartero.   Robert is a mailman.

Nationality:

Ellos son mejicanos.   They are Mexican.

Time expressions:

Son las dos.   It is two o'clock.
Hoy es jueves.   Today is Thursday.

Impersonal expressions plus the infinitive:

Es importante comer.   It is important to eat.
Es necesario jugar y cantar.   It is necessary to play and to sing.

Preceding a predicate noun or pronoun:

Ella es una buena maestra.   She is a good teacher.

Using Estar

The conjugation of the present indicative tense of estar is as follows:

yo estoy	I am	nosotros estamos	We are
tú estás	You are	vosotros estáis	You are
él está	He is	ellos están	They are
ella está	She is	ellas están	They are
usted está	You are	ustedes están	You are

Estar, derived from the Latin verb stare (to stand), expresses the following:

Temporary or permanent location:

¿Dónde está la escuela?   Where is the school?

An accidental or temporary condition:

La mujer está contenta.   The woman is glad.
La muchacha está feliz.   The girl is happy.
El niño está triste.   The boy is sad.

Idioms:

Estar bien.   To be well.
Está bien.   All right; OK.

Certain adjectives change their meanings according to whether *ser* or *estar* is used, depending upon whether characteristic or condition is implied.

	With *ser*	With *estar*
alto	tall, high (essentially)	high (location)
bueno	good, kind (essentially)	good (taste)
callado	quiet (disposition)	silent (temporarily)
cansado	boring, tiresome	tired
ciego	blind (permanently)	blind (temporarily or figuratively)
listo	clever	ready
vivo	lively	alive
malo	wicked	ill

Examples:

El hombre está malo.   The man is ill.
El hombre es malo.   The man is wicked.

REPASO

I.   ¿*Cómo se dice en español?*

1. Where is the farmer? He's in the barn. _____

_____

2. The horse is big and brown. _____

3. The farmer is nice and lively. _____

4. Where are they? They are at home. _____

_____

5. My house is in the city. Where do you live? _____

_____

6. The student is clever and intelligent. _____

7. It is important to drink milk. _____

8. It is necessary to brush your teeth. _____

_____

9. The books are on the desk. _____

10. The teacher is sick today. _____

11. I am Mexican. What are you? _____

12. It is two o'clock. _____

13. Miguel is from Calexico. Where are you from? _____

_____

14. The teacher is sad because Luis is sick today. _____

_____

15. Ana looks pretty today. _____

16. The taco tastes good. _____

17. Ricardo is a mailman and Susana is a nurse. _____

_____

18. My grandfather is old. _____

19. The dog is Alberto's and the cat is Isabela's. _____

_____

20. She is a quiet girl. _____

21. I am happy because all is well. _____

_____

22. Where is Juanito? _____

23. My teeth are in my mouth. _____

24. The dog is lively, but the cat is wicked. _____

_____

25. The stars and the sun are in the sky. _____

_____

II. *Ponga usted la forma correcta de ser o de estar.*

1. El libro _____ de Ramón.

2. Tú _____ enojado.

3. Nosotros _____ morenos.

4. Yo _____ de Tejas.

5. ¿_____ tú de los Estados Unidos?

6. Mi hermano y yo _____ de Nueva York.

7. _____ guapo.

8. Nosotros _____ muy enfermos.

9. Mi amigo _____ en España.

10. Yo _____ muy bien.

11. ¿Dónde _____ el parque?

12. Yo _____ en la tienda.

13. Hoy _____ lunes.

14. _____ las tres.

15. ¿De dónde _____ tú?

III. *Adivinanzas*

La mesa

Está en el comedor,
con cuatro patas,
y en ella todos comemos.

El sol

Es grande y redondo
de rayos dorados;
si no está nublado.

IV. *Juego*

¿Quién soy yo?

This game can be played several ways. It can give the child the opportunity to present himself to the teacher and the teacher the opportunity to listen to the self concept of the child. Or, the teacher may use it for community helpers, or career education by giving characteristics of the person and having the children guess who it is.

V. *Poemas*

El Jardinero

*Mi labor es muy hermosa
y trabajo en el jardín,
cultivo flores preciosas y
entre ellas vivo feliz.*

*El sol y la lluvia y el viento
ayudan a mi labor
y los floricitas pagan
con perfume y color.*

La Bandera mexicana

*Verde, la esperanza amada,
blanca, la inocente vida,
colorado anrojecida
es la llama del amor.*

*¿Cuáles son los colores de la
bandera mexicana?*

VI. *Canciones*

¿Dónde está?

(Tune: "Brother John." Use community helpers; let each child choose
one and respond: *el policía, el bombero, el médico, el lechero, el
cartero)*

*¿Dónde está el bombero?
¿Dónde está el bombero?
¡Aquí estoy!
¡Aquí estoy!
¿Cómo está usted, hoy?
Muy bien, gracias
Siéntese, siéntese.*

Un Ayudante

(Tune: "Did You Ever See A Lassie?")

*Yo deseo ser bombero (policía, cartero, etc.)
Bombero, bombero
Yo deseo ser bombero
¡Bombero soy yo!*

¿Qué comer?

(Tune: "Brother John")

Hoy es lunes,
Hoy es lunes,
¿Qué comer?
¿Qué comer?
Lunes los ejotes,
Lunes los ejotes,
M-m-m-   M-m-m-

Hoy es martes,
Hoy es martes,
¿Qué comer?
¿Qué comer?
Lunes los ejotes,
Martes los camotes,
M-m-m-   M-m-m-

Hoy es miércoles,
Hoy es miércoles,
¿Qué comer?
¿Qué comer?
Lunes los ejotes,
Martes los camotes,
Miércoles las fresas,
M-m-m-   M-m-m-

Hoy es jueves,
Hoy es jueves,
¿Qué comer?
¿Qué comer?
Lunes los ejotes,
Martes los camotes,
Miércoles las fresas,
Jueves las cerezas
M-m-m-   M-m-m-

Hoy es viernes,
Hoy es viernes,
¿Qué comer?
¿Qué comer?
Lunes los ejotes,
Martes los camotes,
Miércoles las fresas,
Jueves las cerezas,
Viernes el pescado
M-m-m-   M-m-m-

Hoy es sábado,
Hoy es sábado,
¿Qué comer?
¿Qué comer?
Lunes los ejotes,
Martes los camotes,
Miércoles las fresas
Jueves las cerezas,
Viernes el pescado,
Sábado helado,
M-m-m-   M-m-m-

Hoy es domingo,
Hoy es domingo,
¿Qué comer?
¿Qué comer?
Algo hay de todo
y de este modo,
Lunes los ejotes,
Martes los camotes,
Miércoles las fresas,
Jueves las cerezas,
Viernes el pescado,
Sábado helado,
¡Ay de mí, ay de mí!

DOMINGO
LUNES
MARTES
MIÉRCOLES
JUEVES
VIERNES
SÁBADO

NUMBERS

Cardinal Numbers

cero	0
uno, -a	1
dos	2
tres	3
cuatro	4
cinco	5
seis	6
siete	7
ocho	8
nueve	9
diez	10
once	11
doce	12
trece	13
catorce	14
quince	15
diez y seis	16
diez y siete	17
diez y ocho	18
diez y nueve	19
veinte	20
veinte y uno	21
veinte y dos	22
treinta	30
treinta y tres	33
cuarenta	40
cuarenta y cuatro	44
cincuenta	50
cincuenta y cinco	55
sesenta	60
sesenta y seis	66
setenta	70
setenta y siete	77
ochenta	80
ochenta y ocho	88
noventa	90
noventa y nueve	99
ciento (cien)	100

ciento uno	*101*
doscientos, -as	*200*
doscientos dos	*202*
trescientos, -as	*300*
trescientos tres	*303*
cuatrocientos, -as	*400*
cuatrocientos cuatro	*404*
quinientos, -as	*500*
quinientos cinco	*505*
seiscientos, -as	*600*
seiscientos seis	*606*
setecientos, -as	*700*
setecientos siete	*707*
ochocientos, -as	*800*
ochocientos ocho	*808*
novecientos, -as	*900*
novecientos nueve	*909*
mil	*1,000*
mil novecientos diez	*1,910*
mil novecientos sesenta y seis	*1,966*
dos mil	*2,000*
dos mil doscientos doce	*2,212*
seis mil	*6,000*
seis mil diez y seis	*6,016*
ocho mil	*8,000*
ocho mil ciento ochenta y ocho	*8,188*
un millón	*1,000,000*
un millón cien mil cien	*1,100,100*

Generally, cardinal numbers are invariable. *Uno* and multiples of *ciento* agree in gender and number with the nouns they modify. *Ciento* used alone before a masculine or feminine noun drops the final syllable *to* and becomes *cien*. *Uno* drops *o* preceding a masculine noun and changes *o* to *a* preceding a feminine noun.

Examples:

cien hombres	<u>100 men</u>
cien mujeres	<u>100 women</u>
doscientas libras	<u>200 lbs.</u>
treinta y un libros	<u>31 books</u>
una maestra	<u>one teacher</u>

Do not use *uno* before *ciento* or *mil*.

Examples:

mil doscientos	<u>1,200</u>
ciento cinco	<u>105</u>

In English we may say <u>one hundred one</u> or <u>one hundred and one</u>, <u>two hundred seventeen</u> or <u>two hundred and seventeen</u>. In Spanish we do not use the conjunction to separate hundreds, thousands, or millions, and the next numeral in a series.

Examples:

ciento quince	<u>115</u>
setecientos diez y ocho	<u>718</u>
doscientos cuarenta	<u>240</u>

Do not count above 1,000 by hundreds as we sometimes do in English.

Examples:

mil ochocientos treinta	<u>1,830</u>
mil quinientos catorce	<u>1,514</u>

In Spanish use the word *millón* as a noun followed by the preposition *de* before an object.

Examples:

un millón de pesos	<u>1 million pesos</u>
dos millones de libros	<u>2 million books</u>

Ordinal Numbers

primero	<u>first</u>	*sexto*	<u>sixth</u>
segundo	<u>second</u>	*séptimo*	<u>seventh</u>
tercero	<u>third</u>	*octavo*	<u>eighth</u>
cuarto	<u>fourth</u>	*noveno*	<u>ninth</u>
quinto	<u>fifth</u>	*décimo*	<u>tenth</u>

Ordinal numbers agree in number and gender with the words they modify. They are seldom used above ten. *Primero* and *tercero* drop *o* before a masculine singluar noun.

Examples:

el primer piso	<u>the first floor</u>
los primeros días	<u>the first days</u>
el segundo hombre	<u>the second man</u>
la segunda mujer	<u>the second woman</u>
el tercer libro	<u>the third book</u>
las terceras copias	<u>the third copies</u>

Use cardinal numbers with all days of the month except the first day.

Examples:

El sábado es el primero de mayo.	Saturday is the first day of May.
Nací el tres de mayo.	I was born on the third of May.
El cinco de mayo es día de fiesta en Mejico.	The fifth of May is a holiday in Mexico.

CALENDAR DIVISIONS

Meses del año (Months of the Year)

enero	January
febrero	February
marzo	March
abril	April
mayo	May
junio	June
julio	July
agosto	August
septiembre	September
octubre	October
noviembre	November
diciembre	December

Días de la semana (Days of the Week)

el domingo	Sunday
el lunes	Monday
el martes	Tuesday
el miércoles	Wednesday
el jueves	Thursday
el viernes	Friday
el sábado	Saturday

Estaciones del año (Seasons of the Year)

la primavera	spring
el verano	summer
el otoño	fall, autumn
el invierno	winter

Do not capitalize Spanish months, days, or seasons.

Use the articles *el* or *los* with days of the week, when the days of the week are not preceded by the adjectives *cada, muchos,* or *pocos,* by a number, or by *ser.*

There are several ways to ask the date, month, or day. The most common expressions are shown below:

¿Cuál es la fecha (de hoy)?	What is the date?
¿A qué fecha estamos?	What is the date?
¿A qué mes estamos?	What month is this?
¿A qué día del mes estamos?	What day of the month is it?
¿Qué día del mes es hoy?	What day of the month is it?
¿A cuántos estamos?	What day of the month is it?

To answer, use the following pattern:

el (date) de (month) de (year)

Examples:

el diez y seis de septiembre de mil ochocientos diez	September 16, 1810
el cuatro de julio de mil setecientos setenta y seis	July 4, 1776
el doce de febrero de mil ochocientos nueve	February 12, 1809
el once de noviembre de mil novecientos diez y nueve	November 11, 1919
el doce de octubre de mil novecientos cuarenta y cinco	October 12, 1945

TIME EXPRESSIONS

Always use ser to tell time. Ser is singular when hora is understood, plural when horas is understood. To express the hour of the day, use ser and the feminine definite article, la or las which agrees with hora or horas understood. Media (half) is feminine, agreeing with hora; cuarto (quarter) is a masculine noun. To express time before the half hour, use y (and); to express time after the half hour, use menos (less) and subtract the number of minutes from the next hour.

Examples:

¿Qué hora es?	What time is it?
Es la una.	It is one o'clock.
Son las dos.	It is two o'clock.
Son las tres y cuarto.	It is 3:15 (a quarter after three).
Son las cinco y media.	It is 5:30.
Son las once menos diez.	It is 10 minutes to 11 (10:50).

Use the following expressions to denote a specific time:

de la mañana	sunrise to noon
de la tarde	noon to sunset
de la noche	sunset to midnight
de la madrugada	midnight to sunrise

Example:

Son las cinco de la tarde.	It is 5 o'clock in the afternoon.

Some other time expressions are:

en punto	exactly
a eso de	at about
a las	at
al mediodía	at noon
Es mediodía.	It is noon.
a media noche	at midnight
Son las seis en punto.	It's exactly six.
a eso de las tres	at about three o'clock
a las tres	at three o'clock

REPASO

I. *Para practicar*

1. It is 11 o'clock. _____

2. It is 1:30 in the afternoon. _____

3. It is 9:25 p.m. _____

4. At 8:30 a.m. _____

5. It is exactly 7:15. _____

6. It is noon. _____

7. It is 12:17. _____

8. At 1:15 a.m. _____

9. It is 10:20. _____

10. It is 2:35. _____

II. *¿Cómo se dice en español?*

    1. What is today's date? _____

    2. Today is June 7, 1973. _____

    3. Today is Tuesday, September 23. _____

    4. What day of the month is it? _____

    5. It is Thursday. _____

    6. January is the first month of the year. _____

        _____

    7. Two hundred and forty teachers work in the school. _____

        _____

    8. The classroom is on the first floor. _____

        _____

    9. Today is Wednesday, August 16, 1967. _____

        _____

   10. It is important to arrive the first of July. _____

        _____

III. *¿Cómo se dice en español?*

    1. 33 men _____

    2. 99 _____

    3. 1,000,000 books _____

    4. 404 women _____

    5. 100 men _____

    6. 1,000 _____

    7. 31 examples _____

    8. 500 toys _____

9. 120 rectangles _____

10. 1974 _____

IV. *Rimas*

Pin-uno pin-dos

Pin-uno, pin-dos, pin-tres,
Pin-cuatro, pin-cinco, pin-seis,
Pin-siete, pin-ocho - pingüino

Uno, dos, tres

Uno, dos, tres.
Uno, dos, tres.
¿Cuántas personas,
Son una, dos, tres?

Uno, dos, tres.
Uno, dos, tres.
Mamá y Papá
Y yo somos tres.

Uno más.
Uno más.
¿Cuántas personas
Son una más?

Uno más.
Uno más.
Ese es el niño,
Y con él son cuatro.

A E I O U

A E I O U
Arbolito de Pirú.
Deseo un dulce
¿Qué deseas tú?

V. Juego

Contemos

*Forme un círculo con los niños y enséñeles
la siguiente rima. Hágales repetir verso
por verso. Cuando los niños hayan
aprendido la rima, se tomarán de la
mano y repetirán la rima mientras
caminan, imitando lo que dicen.*

*Como gigantes caminamos,
uno, dos, tres, cuatro.
Enanitos encontramos,
cinco, seis, siete, ocho.
Pajaritos imitamos,
nueve, diez, once, doce.
Muy despacio regresamos,
trece, catorce, quince,
Y ahora todos nos paramos.*

VI. Number Games

The following verses can be used to teach students numbers.

*Yo soy el farolero
de la puerta del sol
subo la escalera
y enciendo el farol,
luego que lo enciendo,
me pongo a cantar;
dos y dos son cuatro,
cuatro y dos son seis,
seis y dos son ocho,
ocho y ocho, dieciséis,
y ocho, veinticuatro,
y ocho, treinta y dos
más diez que añado,
son cuarenta y dos.*

*Dos y dos son cuatro,
tres y tres son seis,
seis y dos son ocho,
y ocho dieciséis.
Trala, lala, lala, trala, lala, la.
Sin equivocarme, yo ya sé sumar.*

Dos por dos son cuatro,
dos por cinco diez,
seis por cinco treinta,
diez por diez cien.
Trala, lala, lala, trala, lala, la.
Ya voy aprendiendo
a multiplicar.

Oye, farolero, prende
mi farol,
ya hace mucho tiempo que
se puso el sol.
Trala, lala, lala, trala, lala, la.

VII. *Ejercicio*

¿Puede Vd. formar algunos problemas de matemáticas?

Example: *Uno y uno son dos*
Tres y tres son _____
Dos por dos son cuatro
Tres por tres son _____

Continúe: _____

_____

_____

_____

SECTION V

Some Important Irregular Verbs in the Present

Indicative Tense. We have seen that in regular verbs the stem, as obtained by removing the infinitive endings, is the same throughout the conjugation.

In irregular verbs, with a few isolated exceptions, the irregularity is entirely in the stem. Verbal irregularities take several forms. This chatpter will treat both some important irregular verbs and radical changing verbs.

The following verbs are irregular due to stem expansion, stem strengthening, vowel changes, etc. The reason for the structural change will be treated at a later time. At this point, it is most efficient to memorize the following verbs, since they do not follow the regular verb pattern. These verbs have the same key words in English as do all regular present tense verbs (do, does, am, are, and is) plus the meaning of the verb.

dar (to give)
yo doy	I give, I am giving
tú das	You give
él, ella, Vd. da	He, she gives, you give
nosotros damos	We give
vosotros dais	You give
ellos, ellas, Vds. dan	They, you give

decir (to say, to tell)
yo digo	I say, I tell
tú dices	You say
él, ella, Vd. dice	He, she says, you say
nosotros decimos	We say
vosotros decís	You say
ellos, ellas, Vds. dicen	They, you say

hacer (to do, to make)
yo hago	I do, I make
tú haces	You do
él, ella, Vd. hace	He, she does, you do
nosotros hacemos	We do
vosotros hacéis	You do
ellos, ellas, Vds. hacen	They, you do

ir (<u>to go</u>)

yo voy	<u>I go, I am going, I do go</u>
tú vas	<u>You go</u>
él, ella, Vd. va	<u>He, she goes, you go</u>
nosotros vamos	<u>We go</u>
vosotros vais	<u>You go</u>
ellos, ellas, Vds. van	<u>They, you go</u>

When *ir* is followed by "*a*" plus an infinitive, it has the future meaning "to be going to do something."

Examples:

Voy a leer un cuento.	<u>I am going to read a story.</u>
Ella va a borrar el pizarrón.	<u>She is going to erase the blackboard.</u>

oír (<u>to hear</u>)

yo oigo	<u>I hear, I do hear</u>
tú oyes	<u>You hear</u>
él, ella, Vd. oye	<u>He, she hears, you hear</u>
nosotros oímos	<u>We hear</u>
vosotros oís	<u>You hear</u>
ellos, ellas, Vds. oyen	<u>They, you hear</u>

poner (<u>to put, to place</u>)

yo pongo	<u>I put, place, I do put</u>
tú pones	<u>You put</u>
él, ella, Vd. pone	<u>He, she puts, you put</u>
nosotros ponemos	<u>We put</u>
vosotros ponéis	<u>You put</u>
ellos, ellas, Vds. ponen	<u>They, you put</u>

saber (<u>to know</u> [a thing])

yo sé	<u>I know</u>
tú sabes	<u>You know</u>
él, ella, Vd. sabe	<u>He, she knows, you know</u>
nosotros sabemos	<u>We know</u>
vosotros sabéis	<u>You know</u>
ellos, ellas, Vds. saben	<u>They, you know</u>

When *saber* is followed by an infinitive, it has the meaning "to know how to."

Examples:

El niño sabe contar en español.	<u>The child knows how to count in Spanish.</u>
Los niños saben dibujar la bandera mejicana.	<u>The children know how to draw the Mexican flag.</u>

tener (to have)

yo tengo	I have
tú tienes	You have
él, ella, Vd. tiene	He, she has, you have
nosotros tenemos	We have
vosotros tenéis	You have
ellos, ellas, Vds. tienen	They, you have

ver (to see)

yo veo	I see
tú ves	You see
él, ella, Vd. ve	He, she sees, you see
nosotros vemos	We see
vosotros veis	You see
ellos, ellas, Vds. ven	They, you see

venir (to come)

yo vengo	I come
tú vienes	You come
él, ella, Vd. viene	He, she comes, you come
nosotros venimos	We come
vosotros venís	You come
ellos, ellas, Vds. vienen	They, you come

REPASO

I. *Use Vd. un ejemplo de cada verbo en una frase que aplica a su propio trabajo. ¡Es importante usar vocabulario nuevo!*

II. *¿Cómo se dice en español?*

1. We hear the song. _____

2. Do you know how to speak Spanish? _____

   _____

3. The teacher gives the eraser to (*a*) Juan and he goes to the

   blackboard. _____

   _____

4. We are going to the store. _____

5. I put the book on the desk because I don't know how to read.

   _____

6. We are making a *piñata* for the party. _____

_____

7. The children see the flowers when they come to our class.

_____

8. I don't know if he has a brother. _____

_____

9. Do you have toys at home? _____

10. Where do we put the paper? _____

11. What is the teacher doing? _____

12. She is putting the hat on the clown. _____

_____

13. When are we going to sing? _____

14. I don't hear the music now. _____

15. What are the children saying? _____

16. What are you going to buy? _____

17. I'm going to buy bread in the bakery. _____

_____

18. We are going to learn English. _____

19. What time is it? _____

20. Does she have a friend? _____

Using *Tener* Idiomatically

The verb *tener* means <u>to have</u> and is irregular in the present tense. To review, the conjugation of *tener* is:

yo tengo	<u>I have</u>	*nosotros tenemos*	<u>We have</u>
tú tienes	<u>You have</u>	*vosotros tenéis*	<u>You have</u>
ella tiene	<u>She has</u>	*ellos tienen*	<u>They have</u>
él tiene	<u>He has</u>	*Vds. tienen*	<u>You (pl) have</u>
Vd. tiene	<u>You have</u>		

Tener expresses possession and age.

Tengo mucho dinero.	I have a lot of money.
La mujer tiene dos niños.	The woman has two children.
¿Cuántos años tiene usted?	How old are you?
Tengo veinte años.	I am 20 years old.
El niño tiene cinco años.	The boy is five.

Use *tener* idiomatically with a personal subject and certain nouns. When English expresses <u>to be</u>, Spanish uses <u>to have</u>.

Examples:

tener calor (m)	to be warm
tener cuidado (m)	to be careful
tener la culpa (f)	to be at fault, to be guilty
tener frío (m)	to be cold
tener hambre (f)	to be hungry
tener miedo (m)	to be afraid
tener prisa (f)	to be in a hurry
tener razón (f)	to be right
tener sed (f)	to be thirsty
tener sueño (m)	to be sleepy
no tener razón (f)	to be wrong
¿Qué tienes?	What's wrong? What's the matter?

With *que* and an infinitive, *tener* denotes a strong obligation or necessity and means <u>to have to</u> or <u>must</u> with a subject. The verb following *tener que* must always be in the infinitive form.

Examples:

Tienes que hablar español.	You must speak Spanish.
Vds. tienen que comprar pan en la panadería.	You must buy bread in the bakery.

Using *Hay Que* Idiomatically

When the expression denoting necessity is used impersonally (without a subject), you may use *hay que* plus an infinitive to mean <u>one must</u> or <u>it is necessary to</u>.

Examples:

Hay que estudiar en la escuela.	It is necessary to study in school.
Hay que comer para vivir.	One must eat (in order) to live.

Using *Hacer* Idiomatically

Hacer is also used idiomatically with certain expressions where English uses <u>to be</u>. Expressions of weather are frequently used with *hacer* in its third person singular form.

Examples:

¿Qué tiempo hace?	<u>How's the weather?</u>
Hace (mucho) frío.	<u>It's (very) cold.</u>
Hace (mucho) calor.	<u>It's (very) warm.</u>
Hace (mucho) sol.	<u>It's (very) sunny.</u>
Hace (mucho) viento.	<u>It's (very) windy.</u>
Hace fresco.	<u>It's cool.</u>
Hace buen tiempo.	<u>It's nice weather.</u>

Some classroom expressions commonly used with *hacer* are:

	hacer caso a	<u>to pay attention to</u>
	hacer cola	<u>to stand in line</u>
Examples:	Luis hace caso a la lección.	<u>Luis pays attention to the lesson.</u>
	Los niños hacen cola.	<u>The children are standing in line.</u>

REPASO

I. ¿Cómo se dice en español?

1. What's the matter, Daniel? _____

2. It is necessary to brush your teeth. _____

    _____

3. In May it is nice weather and you don't have to wear a coat.

    _____

4. The man has to buy milk in the store. _____

    _____

5. One must eat to (*para*) live. _____

6. Are you afraid, Gloria? _____

7. How old are you, Ramón? _____

8. I'm six, señorita. _____

9. One must listen to (*para*) learn. _____

10. You must speak Spanish in the class. _____

_____

11. When it's warm weather, I'm always sleepy. _____

_____

12. We are thirsty and hungry. _____

13. It is windy and cold in March and I'm always cold in the class.

_____

14. Today is Monday and it is warm and sunny. _____

_____

15. They are standing in line near the door. _____

_____

16. You must pay attention to the teacher. _____

_____

17. You must wear a jacket when it's cold (weather). _____

_____

18. It is ten o'clock and I'm very sleepy. _____

_____

19. We are going to play and you must form a circle. _____

_____

20. Do you have a brother? How old is he? _____

_____

II. *Adivinanzas*

Si soy joven, joven quedo
Si soy viejo, quedo viejo
tengo boca y no hablo
tengo ojos y no veo.
(El retrato)

Tengo mi carita blanca
redondita y luminosa,
hago los campos de plata
y las noches muy hermosas.
(La luna)

III. *Trabalenguas* (Tongue Twisters)

R con R cigarro,
R con R barril
Rápido corren los carros,
allí en el ferrocarril.

A mí me mima, mi mamá,
Mi mamá a mí me mima.

Pablito clavó un clavito
un clavito clavó Pablito.

IV. *Juego*

A-E-I-O-U

Arbolito de Perú,
Yo tengo seis años
¿Cuántos años tienes tú?

Los meses del año

Treinta días tiene noviembre
Treinta abril, junio y septiembre
Veintiocho, tiene uno
y los demás treinta y uno.

V. *Canción*

La manzanita[1]

En esta casa roja, roja, roja,
en esta casa roja vivo yo,
en esta manzanita, manzanita
en esta manzanita vivo yo.
Tiene una chimenea, chimenea
tiene una chimenea color café,
yo sé que es muy bonita mi casita,
yo sé que es muy bonita yo lo sé.

Tecolote (Poor Little Owl)

Tecolote,
tienes hambre, pajarito
cu, cu, cu.
Te-cu, tu-cu, cu-cu,
te-cu, tu-cu, cu-cu.
Pobrecito pajarito,
tienes hambre, tecolotito
cu, cu, cu.

Diez gallinitas

Cinco huevitos
y cinco huevitos
son diez.

La gallina se pone
sobre de ellos
otra vez.

Pío, pío, pío.

¿Qué ves?

Diez pollitos
Esta vez.

---

[1]Carol Perkins in Information and Materials to Teach the Cultural Heritage of the Mexican-American Child. November, 1972. (Education Service Center, Region XIII, Austin, Texas), p. 91.

VI. *Un cuento*

Caperucita Roja

En una casa situada en un bosque vive una niña con su madre y su padre. La niña se llama Caperucita Roja. Al otro lado del bosque vive su abuela.

Un día, la madre llama a la niña, --Caperucita Roja, CAPERUCITA ROJA.

--Sí, mamá.

--Caperucita Roja, tu abuela está enferma. Toma esta cesta. Es comida.

--Sí, mamá.

--¡Pero, cuidado! Hay un lobo en el bosque.

--Bueno, mamá. -- Y la niña corre al bosque con la cesta.

En el bosque el lobo está sentado al lado del camino. El lobo dice, --Tengo habre.

Cuando el lobo ve a la niña, el lobo dice, --Buenos días, niña. ¿A dónde vas?

--Voy a la casa de mi abuela con esta cesta de comida,-- dice la niña.

--Ay,-- dice el lobo. --¿Está enferma la abuela?

--Sí,-- dice la niña.

--¿Dónde vive la abuela?-- dice el lobo.

--Mi abuela vive al otro lado del bosque,-- dice la niña.

--Ah, sí,-- dice el lobo. --Buenos días, niña.

Y la niña va por el camino. El lobo corre por el bosque a la casa de la abuela. El lobo llama a la puerta de la casa.

--¿Quién llama?-- dice la abuela.

--Soy yo. Soy Caperucita Roja. Tengo una cesta de comida,-- dice el lobo.

--Entra,-- dice la abuela.

El lobo entra en la casa. La abuela esta acostada en la cama. El lobo dice, --¡Tengo hambre!

--¡Ay! ¡Ay!-- dice la abuela. --Tengo mucho miedo. ¡Usted es el lobo!-- Y la abuela corre por el bosque.

El lobo se acuesta en la cama de la abuela. Caperucita Roja va a la casa y llama a la puerta.

--Abuela,-- dice Caperucita Roja.

--¿Quién llama?-- dice el lobo en la voz de la abuela.

--Soy yo. Soy Caperucita Roja,-- dice la niña. --Tengo una cesta de comida.

--Entra,-- dice el lobo en voz de la abuela.

La niña entra en la casa, y el lobo se cubre con la ropa de la cama.

--Buenos días, Caperucita Roja,-- dice el lobo.

--Aquí está la cesta de comida.

--Muchas gracias, Caperucita Roja.

--Ay, abuela,-- dice la niña. --Está usted muy enferma.

--Sí, niña,-- dice el lobo.

--Abuela, ¿por qué tiene usted los ojos tan grandes?

--Para ver a mi niña,-- dice el lobo.

--Abuela, ¿por qué tiene usted las orejas tan grandes?

--Para oír a mi niña,-- dice el lobo.

--Abuela, ¿por qué tiene usted los dientes tan enormes?

--Para COMER A MI NIÑA,-- dice el lobo.

--¡Ay! ¡Ay!-- dice la niña. --¡Usted es el lobo! ¡Tengo mucho miedo! ¡Socorro! ¡Socorro!

En ese momento, la abuela vuelve del bosque con el padre y su perro.

--¡Socorro!-- dice Caperucita Roja.

El padre entra en la casa con su perro.

--¡Socorro!-- dice el lobo. --¡Es un PERRO! ¡Socorro!

El lobo corre por el bosque y nunca, nunca, nunca, regresa a la casa de la abuela.

SECTION VI

ARTICLES

In Spanish, as in English, there are definite and indefinite articles.

Indefinite Articles

In English we determine the form of the indefinite article by the first letter of the following word (a before words beginning with a consonant, an before words beginning with a vowel), but in Spanish it is the last sound of the word which tells us to use *un* or *una*.

	Singular		Plural	
Masculine	*un*	a, an	*unos*	some, a few
Feminine	*una*	a, an	*unas*	some, a few

Definite Articles

While in English there is only one form of the definite article, the, in Spanish there are four forms (and a neuter).

	Singular		Plural	
Masculine	*el*	the	*los*	the
Feminine	*la*	the	*las*	the
Neuter	*lo*	the		

Usage. The leading difference between the Spanish and the English use of the definite article is that it is employed in Spanish before any noun used in a general sense.

Examples:

El pan es nutritivo.	Bread is nutritious.
Los caballos son animales útiles.	Horses are useful animals.

When a noun is used partitively (to represent "some"), the article is omitted.

Example:

Quiero agua.	I want (some) water.

Before all titles (except *Don, Doña, Fray, Santa*) the definite article is required when the individual is spoken of, but not when he is addressed.

Examples:

La señora Medina abre la puerta.	Mrs. Medina opens the door.
"Buenos días, Señora Medina."	"Good day, Mrs. Medina."

Contractions

a + el = al	to the
de + el = del	from the, of the

These contractions do not occur when the article is part of a proper name. For example: *a El Escorial; de El Buscón.*

Agreement of Articles

Generally, use an article before each noun and make it agree in gender and number with the noun.

Examples:

la familia	the family
las familias	the families
los amigos	the friends
un pollo	a chicken
una galleta	a cookie
unas hamburguesas	some hamburgers

For euphony, use *el* not *la* immediately preceding a feminine singular noun which begins with a stressed *a* or *ha*. The gender of the noun remains feminine.

Examples:

el agua	the water (f)
but	
las aguas	the waters
el alma	the soul (f)
but	
las almas	the souls
la ayudante	the helper, assistant (where the first a is not stressed)

NOUNS

Gender

Spanish nouns are either masculine or feminine. Generally, names of things ending in *-o* are masculine, and feminine if they end in *-a*.

Examples:

un juego	a game
una adivinanza	a riddle

Nouns ending in *-ad, -ud, -ie, -ión,* and *-umbre* are usually feminine.

Examples:

la amistad	friendship
la canción	song
la juventud	youth
la serie	series
la legumbre	vegetable

Regardless of word endings, nouns denoting female beings are feminine; nouns denoting male beings are masculine.

Examples:

un hombre	a man
una mujer	a woman

Nouns designating days, months, and languages are masculine.

Examples:

el viernes	Friday
el español	Spanish
el lunes	Monday

The gender of certain nouns does not conform to these rules and must be learned. A dictionary indicates whether these nouns are feminine (f) or masculine (m).

Examples:

nariz (f); una nariz	a nose
mano (f); la mano	the hand

Plural Noun Forms

To form a noun's plural, add *-s* or *-es* to the singular. Nouns ending in an unstressed vowel add *-s* to form the plural.

Examples:

brazo	<u>arm</u>
brazos	<u>arms</u>
oso	<u>bear</u>
osos	<u>bears</u>

Nouns ending in a consonant or *-y*, add *-es* to form the plural.

Examples:

animal	<u>animal</u>
animales	<u>animals</u>
buey	<u>ox</u>
bueyes	<u>oxen</u>

Nouns of more than one syllable ending in a stressed *e, o, u,* add *-s* to form the plural. Apply the same rule to monosyllables.

Examples:

tisú	<u>tissue</u>
tisús	<u>tissues</u>
pie	<u>foot</u>
pies	<u>feet</u> ·

Nouns which end in stressed *a* or *i* or a stressed dipthong of which the last letter is *-y*, add *-es*.

Examples:

rubí	<u>ruby</u>
rubíes	<u>rubies</u>
rey	<u>king</u>
reyes	<u>kings</u>

Nouns ending in *-z*, change *-z* to *-c* before adding *-es* to form the plural. This retains the singular sound in the plural noun form.

Examples:

lápiz	<u>pencil</u>
lápices	<u>pencils</u>

Nouns ending in unstressed *-es* or *-is*, add no ending. Plurality is expressed by the articles.

Examples:

el lunes	Monday (or "on Monday")
los lunes	Mondays (or "on Mondays")

OBJECT PRONOUNS

Object pronouns are pronouns used as the verb's direct or indirect objects. A direct object answers who or what; an indirect object answers to whom or for whom. They have a direct correspondence to the personal pronouns.

Personal Pronouns

yo	I
tú	you (familiar singular)
él	he
ella	she
usted (*Vd., Ud.*)	you (polite singular)
nosotros	we
vosotros	you (familiar plural)
ellos	they
ellas	they
ustedes (*Vds., Uds.*)	you (polite plural)

Indirect and Direct Object Pronouns

Indirect Object Pronouns

me	me, to me
te	you, to you (familiar singular)
le	him, to him
le	her, to her
le	you, to you
nos	us, to us
os	you, to you (familiar plural)
les	them, to them
les	them, to them
les	you, to you (polite plural)

Direct Object Pronouns

me	me
te	you (familiar singular)
le, lo	him, it (m), you
la	her, you (f), it (f)
le	you (m)
nos	us
vos	you (familiar plural)
los	them (m)
las	them (f), you (pl f)
los	you (polite plural)
les	you (pl), them (m) (frequently used in Spain)

When it is necessary to clarify *le* or *les*, use *a él, a ella, a usted, a ellos, a ellas,* or *a ustedes* after the verb. In the masculine singular when referring to persons both *le* and *lo* are used. *Lo* is more common in Mexico; *le* is more common in Spain. *Lo* is also used to refer to things of the masculine gender.

Examples:

Le veo en la escuela.	I see him in school.
Lo veo en la escuela.	I see him/it in school.

Use *la* to indicate feminine persons and things.

Usage and Placement

Object pronouns usually precede the verb.

Examples:

Me enseña el español.	He is teaching me Spanish.
Le enseño a él el español.	I am teaching him Spanish.

However, if the verb is in the form of the infinitive, present participle, or positive imperative, attach the pronoun objects to the end of the verb.

Examples:

Tengo que hablarle.	I must speak to him.
Está estudiándolo.	He is studying it.
Dígalo en español.	Say it in Spanish.

If there are two pronoun objects--direct object and an indirect object-- they both precede or follow the verb according to the above rules, and the indirect object precedes the direct object.

Examples:

Me lo dice.	He tells me it. (indirect object, direct object, verb)
Desea decírmelo.	He wants to tell me it.

If there are two personal pronoun objects, both of the third person, change the indirect object *le* or *les* to *se* and clarify *se* by the addition of *a* plus a personal pronoun (*a él, a ella, a usted, a ellos, a ellas,* or *a ustedes*).

Examples:

Se lo dice a él.	He tells it to him.
El no desea decírselo a ella.	He doesn't want to tell it to her.

When the verb's direct object is a noun not a pronoun, use the preposition *a* only if the object denotes a specific person. Do not translate *a* in English.

Examples:

     (Le) Veo a Juan.   <u>I see John.</u>
     Lo veo.   <u>I see him.</u>

Always use the preposition *a* when the verb's object is indirect.

Examples:

     (Le) Escribo a Juan.   <u>I write to John.</u>
     Le escribo a él.   <u>I write to him.</u>

REPASO

I.   *¿Cómo se dice en español?*

    1. They see us. _____

    2. We see them. _____

    3. Do you hear me? _____

    4. He paints it. _____

    5. I have a letter and she is going to see it. _____

        _____

    6. He tells it to her. _____

    7. The teacher gives him the chalk. _____

        _____

    8. Here are the blocks. You must put them in a circle. _____

        _____

    9. The little boy doesn't want to tell him it. _____

        _____

   10. When we have money, we eat in a restaurant. _____

        _____

11. Are you thirsty? _____

12. When I go to the dentist, he asks me if I have a toothbrush.

_____

13. You have to go to the cafeteria now. _____

_____

14. How old are you? I'm six. _____

_____

15. The baker makes bread and we buy it in the bakery. _____

_____

16. The mailman gives me the letters and I put them in the mailbox.

_____

17. The policeman helps us. _____

18. It is important to wait for the traffic light. _____

_____

19. Where are you from? _____

20. Do you live in a house? I want to see it. _____

_____

II. *Un drama*

El Flautista De Jamelín

En el pueblo de Jamelín hay muchas casas. En las casas hay muchos hombres y muchas mujeres y muchos niños. Pero el pueblo de Jamelín está muy triste porque en las casas hay muchas ratas.

Todos los días las mujeres dicen, --¡Ay, qué tristes estamos! ¿Por qué tenemos tantas ratas en este pueblo de Jamelín?

Los niños dicen a las mujeres, --¿Por qué no echan las ratas del pueblo?

Y las mujeres dicen a los hombres, --¿Por qué no echan las ratas del pubelo?

Y los hombres van al alcalde y dicen, --¿Por qué no echa las ratas del pueblo?

Y el alcalde dice, --No puedo.

Y todo el pueblo está muy triste.

Un día, un flautista llega al pueblo.

--¡Qué pueblo tan triste!-- dice el flautista.

--Sí,-- dicen los niños. --Tenemos muchas ratas en el pueblo.

--¿Por qué no echan las ratas del pueblo?-- dice el flautista.

--Las mujeres no pueden,-- dicen los niños. --Los hombres no pueden, ni el alcalde puede.

--Ah,-- dice el flautista. El flautista piensa. El flautista va al alcalde, y dice, --Su pueblo tiene muchas ratas.

--Sí,-- dice el alcalde, muy triste.

--¿Por qué no echan las ratas del pueblo?-- dice el flautista.

--No puedo echarlas,-- dice el alcalde.

--Págame cien pesos,-- dice el flautista, --y yo echo las ratas del pueblo.

--Bueno,-- dice el alcalde. --Eche las ratas del pueblo, y yo le pago cien pesos.

El flautista va por las calles del pueblo. Toca su flauta. Las ratas salen de las casas y siguen al flautista. El flautista va tocando por el camino y las ratas le siguen al bosque. ¡Qué alegre está el pueblo! En las casas no hay ratas. Los niños están alegres. Las mujeres están alegres. Los hombres están alegres. Pero el alcalde está muy triste.

--Yo tengo que pagar al flautista cien pesos,-- dice el alcalde. --Estoy my triste.

Al fin, el flautista vuelve al pueblo, y va al alcalde. --Págame cien pesos,-- dice el flautista.

Pero el alcalde piensa, y dice, --Flautista, ahora no hay ratas en el pueblo de Jamelín. No le pago cien pesos.

--No es un hombre honrado,-- dice el flautista. --El pueblo de Jamelín va a estar muy triste.

El flautista va por las calles del pueblo y toca su flauta. Los niños salen de las casas y siguen al flautista. El flautista va tocando por el camino y los niños le siguen al bosque.

¡Qué triste está el pueblo! Los hombres van al alcalde, y dicen, --¿Dónde están los niños? ¡Usted tiene la culpa! ¡No es un hombre honrado!

--Pero no hay ratas en las casas,-- dice el alcalde.

--Sí, no hay ratas en las casas, pero ¡no hay niños, tampoco! Y los hombres están muy tristes.

Al fin, una mujer dice, --El alcalde dice que no hay ratas en el pueblo.

--Sí,-- dicen los otras mujeres.

--Pero hay una rata,-- dice la mujer.

--¿Dónde está la rata?-- dicen las otras mujeres.

--Vamos,-- dicen la mujer. Y todas las mujeres la siguen.

--¡Aquí está la rata!-- dice la mujer. --¡Es el alcalde! ¡No es un hombre honrado!

--Sí, sí,-- dicen las otras mujeres. --¿Dónde están los niños?

Y las mujeres echan al alcalde del pueblo de Jamelín. En ese momento, el flautista vuelve del bosque.

--¿Dónde está el alcalde?-- dice el flautista.

--Le hemos echado del pueblo,-- dicen las mujeres.

--Bueno, bueno,-- dice el flautista. --El alcalde no es un hombre honrado.

--Pero somos hombres honrados,-- dicen los hombres del pueblo. Le pagamos cien pesos.

Hay cien hombres en el pueblo. Todos los hombres pagan un peso.

--Aquí están los cien pesos,-- dicen los hombres.

El flautista va por el camino, y vuelve con los niños. --Yo tengo mis cien pesos,-- dice el flautista. --Aquí están los niños.

Y no hay ratas en las casas del pueblo. Y al fin el pueblo está muy alegre. Pero el alcalde vive en el bosque con las ratas y nunca, nunca, nunca, vuelve al pueblo de Jamelín.

Preguntas sobre - _El Flautista de Jamelín_

1. ¿Por qué está triste el pueblo de Jamelín?

2. ¿Qué va a hacer el flautista?

3. ¿Cómo va a hacerlo?

4. ¿Cómo están los niños, los hombres y las mujeres después del flautista?

5. ¿Quién está triste y por qué?

6. Cuando el alcalde dice que no va a pagarle, ¿qué hace el flautista?

7. ¿Cómo están los hombres y las mujeres?

8. ¿Qué hacen las mujeres?

9. ¿Quiénes le pagan al flautista?

10. Al fin, ¿qué le pasa al flautista?

III. _Poema_

Aserrín, Aserrán

Aserrín, Aserrán,
Los maderos de San Juan,
Piden pan, no les dan,
Piden queso, les dan hueso
Y les cortan el pescueso.

Aserrín, Asserrán
Los maderos de San Juan
Piden pan, no les dan
Piden papa, les dan nata
Y les cortan la corbata.

Aserrín, Aserrán,
Los maderos de San Juan,
Piden pan, no les dan,
Piden ardejas, les dan viejas
Y les cortan las orejas.

Aserrín, Aserrán,
Los maderos de San Juan
Piden pan, no les dan
Piden un peso, les dan ceso
Y les cortan el bostezo.

Aserrín, Aserrán,
Los maderos de San Juan
Piden pan, no les dan
Piden pato, les dan gato
Y les cortan los zapatos.

Aserrín, Aserrán,
Los maderos de San Juan
Piden pan, no les dan
Piden araña, les dan caña
Y les cortan las pestañas.

La Vaca

Gracias amiguita vaca
por la leche que nos das,
por la buena mantequilla
que comemos con el pan.

Por la carne y por los pieles
Y por otras cosas más
con que siempre nos regalas,
buena vaca del corral.

IV. Canción

Looby Lou

Vamos a jugar,
Vamos a jugar,
Vamos a jugar,
Vamos a jugar.

Meto la mano derecha,
Saco la mano derecha,
Sacudo la mano, así, así,
Y salto alrededor.

Vamos a jugar, etc.

Meto la mano izquierda,
Saco la mano izquierda,
Sacudo la mano, así, así,
Y salto alrededor.

Vamos a jugar, etc.

Meto el pie derecho,
Saco el pie derecho,
Sacudo el pie, así, así,
Y salto alrededor.

Vamos a jugar, etc.

Meto el pie izquierdo,
Saco el pie izquierdo,
Sacudo el pie, así, así,
Y salto alrededor.

Vamos a jugar, etc.

Meto la cabeza,
Saco la cabeza,
Sacudo la cabeza, así, así,
Y salto alrededor.

Vamos a jugar, etc.

Meto todo el cuerpo,
Saco todo el cuerpo,
Sacudo el cuerpo, así, así,
Y salto alrededor.

Adjectives as Modifiers

An adjective serves to modify a noun and it agrees in number and gender with the noun it modifies. While in English an adjective precedes a noun, in Spanish it may both precede and follow depending on its function. An adjective takes a plural inflection in Spanish when the noun it modifies is plural. This phenomenon does not occur in English.

Adjectives ending in *-o* in the masculine singular change *-o* to *-a* to form the feminine.

Examples:

el bloque rojo	the red block
la pelota roja	the red ball

Use the plural form of an adjective if it modifies a plural noun or several nouns.

Follow the same rules for forming plural adjectives as for forming plural nouns. (See previous chapter for review.)

Examples:

los creyones rojos	the red crayons
las casas rojas	the red houses

If some nouns are masculine and some are feminine, use a masculine plural adjective.

Example:

los árboles y las flores bonitos	the pretty trees and flowers

Adjestives not ending in *-o* usually have the same form for both genders.

Examples:

un pájaro azul	a bluebird
una blusa azul	a blue blouse
unas gorras azules	some blue caps
unos sombreros azules	some blue hats

Adjectives ending in a consonant and denoting nationality add -a to form the feminine.

Examples:

español	*española*	<u>Spanish</u>
inglés	*inglesa*	<u>English</u>

Possessive Adjectives

The full inflection of possessive adjectives is given below. *Mi, tu,* and *su* have one form for both genders; *nuestro* and *vuestro* vary as do all adjectives ending in *-o*.

Singular	Plural	
mi	*mis*	<u>my</u>
tu	*tus*	<u>your</u> (familiar)
su	*sus*	<u>his, her, your, their, its</u>
nuestro, -a	*nuestros, -as*	<u>our</u>
vuestro, -a	*vuestros, -as*	<u>your</u> (familiar)

Since *su* and *sus* have so many meanings, it is often necessary to use the preposition *de* and the proper prepositional pronoun after the object possessed. The prepositional pronouns are the same as the personal pronouns with the exception of the first and second person singular. When the personal pronoun is *yo*, the prepositional pronoun is *mí* and when the personal pronoun is *tú*, the prepositional pronoun is *ti*. When using the prepositional pronoun for clarity, generally substitute the definite article for the possessive adjective.

Examples:

su silla	<u>your chair, his chair, her chair</u>
la silla de usted	<u>your chair</u>
la silla de él	<u>his chair</u>
su libro	<u>his book, her book, your book, their book</u>
el libro de él	<u>his book</u>
el libro de ellos	<u>their book</u>

The possessive adjective agrees in number and gender with the noun it modifies, not with the possessor.

Examples:

mi amigo	<u>my friend</u>
mis amigos	<u>my friends</u>
su bicicleta	<u>his, her, their, your bicycle</u>
nuestro burro	<u>our donkey</u>
nuestra bandera	<u>our flag</u>
nuestros discos	<u>our records</u>

With parts of the body and articles of clothing, use a definite article, not a possessive adjective.

Examples:

Voy a ponerme el abrigo.	I'm going to put on my coat.
Es necesario cepillar los dientes.	It is necessary to brush your teeth.

There is no possessive case of nouns in Spanish. In English an apostrophe s ('s) is used for this function. To express possession in Spanish, use *de* before the possessor.

Examples:

el brazo de María	Maria's arm
el perro del niño	the boy's dog

Demonstrative Adjectives

Singular		Plural	
este, esta	this	*estos, estas*	these
ese, esa	that	*esos, esas*	those
aquel, aquella	that	*aquellos, aquellas*	those

Demonstrative adjectives agree in number and gender with the nouns modified.

Examples:

ese gato	that cat
esos gatos	those cats

Repeat demonstrative and possessive adjectives before each noun to which they refer.

Examples:

este cuchillo y esta cuchara	this knife and spoon
mi madre y mi padre	my mother and father

Ese, esa, esos, and *esas* are used when referring to an object near the person speaking. *Aquel, aquella, aquellos,* and *aquellas* are used when referring to an object far from the speaker.

Demonstrative adjectives standing alone take the place of the object pointed out and bear an accent mark over the vowel of the proper syllable. Standing alone, they are demonstrative pronouns and agree in number and gender with the nouns they replace.

Examples:

El niño dibuja con ese creyón.	<u>The boy draws with that crayon.</u>
El niño dibuja con ése.	<u>The boy draws with that one.</u>
Ellos forman un conjunto con aquellos palos.	<u>They form a set with those sticks.</u>
Ellos forman un conjunto con aquéllos.	<u>They form a set with those.</u>

Comparative Adjectives

There are three degrees of comparison: the positive, the comparative, and the superlative. In English the adjective is compared by adding <u>-er</u> (comparative) and <u>-est</u> (superlative) to the positive form or by placing <u>more</u> or <u>less</u> (comparative) and <u>most</u> or <u>least</u> (superlative) before the positive form.

In Spanish adjectives are compared by placing *más* (more) or *menos* (less) before the positive form. The superlative form of the adjective is the same as the comparative, but the noun is modified by the definite article.

Positive	Comparative	Superlative
inteligente	*más inteligente*	*el más inteligente*
	menos inteligente	*el menos inteligente*

The superlative form of the adjective usually follows the noun.

Example:

El chico más inteligente de la clase es Juan.

The word for <u>in</u> following a superlative is *de.*

The following four adjectives are compared irregularly:

bueno (good)	*mejor* (better)	*el mejor* (best)
malo (bad)	*peor* (worse)	*el peor* (worst)
grande (old)	*mayor* (older)	*el mayor* (oldest)
pequeño (young)	*menor* (younger)	*el menor* (youngest)

Both *grande* and *pequeño* are also compared regularly. When compared irregularly they refer to age; when compared regularly, they refer to size.

The word <u>than</u> is expressed in Spanish by *que* except:

1. Before numerals, <u>than</u> is expressed by *de.*

Example:

El niño sabe más de diez números.   <u>The child knows more than 10 numbers.</u>

2. But, in negative sentences, *no más que* translates <u>only</u>.

Example:

El niño no sabe más que	<u>The child only knows 10 numbers.</u>
diez números.	OR . . . <u>knows only 10 numbers.</u>

The comparative of equality (as . . . as) is expressed in Spanish by (*tan* + adjective + *como*) or (*tanto* + noun + *como*).

Examples:

Este libro es tan	<u>This book is as interesting as</u>
interesante como ése.	<u>that one.</u>
Tiene tantos libros como	<u>He has as many books as you.</u>
tú.	

Adjective Placement

A descriptive adjective follows the noun it modified.

Examples:

el juguete roto	<u>the broken toy</u>
la mujer gorda	<u>the fat lady</u>

Limiting, demonstrative, and possessive adjectives precede the noun modified.

Examples:

dos gusanos	<u>two worms</u>
mucho ruido	<u>much noise, a lot of noise</u>
este triángulo	<u>this triangle</u>
mi hermano	<u>my brother</u>

Adverbs

Adverbs are words expressing time, place, manner, degree, affirmation or negation. They modify adjectives, verbs, or adverbs and are invariable in form. To form an adverb from an adjective, add the ending *-mente* to the <u>feminine</u> form of the adjective. If the adjective ends in a consonant, simply add *-mente* to the end.

Examples:

seria	<u>serious</u>
seriamente	<u>seriously</u>
fácil	<u>easy</u>
fácilmente	<u>easily</u>

If two or more adverbs occur together, add *–mente* to the last adjective only.

Example:

Ella habla lenta y cuidadosamente.	<u>She speaks slowly and carefully.</u>

Adverbs are also commonly formed by *con* (<u>with</u>) and a noun.

Example:

con cuidado	<u>carefully</u>

Adverbs generally follow the verb in a sentence.

Example:

La maestra habla rápidamente.	<u>The teacher speaks rapidly.</u>

Comparison of Adverbs

Adverbs use the same formula as adjectives to express comparisons of equality or inequality. Some formulas for comparison of adverbs are:

tan + adverb + *como* = comparison of equality;

Example:

Juanito habla tan bien como yo.	<u>Juanito speaks as well as I (do).</u>

más + adverb + *que* = comparison of inequality;

Example:

Llego a la escuela más tarde que Ana.	<u>I arrive at school later than Ana.</u>

menos + adverb + *que* = comparison of inequality.

The adverbs *bien, mal, mucho* and *poco* have special forms for comparisons of inequality: *mejor* (better, the best), *peor* (worse, the worst), *más* (more, the most), *menos* (less, the least). These forms are also used as superlatives.

Diminutives

A diminutive is a word formed from another by the addition of an ending expressing smallness in size and sometimes endearment or contempt. A diminutive gives some words a very different connotation and the most common word ending in Spanish is *-ito* and its variations. Certain areas of the Spanish-speaking world prefer to use *-ico* and *-illo*.

1. Words ending in *-o* or *-a*, replace those endings with *-ito* or *-ita* (for example: *Juana* → *Juanita*).

2. Words ending in any consonant except n̄ or r̄, directly attach *-ito* or *-ita* (for example: *español* → *españolita*).

3. Words whose singular ends in *-e*, *-n*, or *-r*, directly attach the ending *-cito* or *-cita* (for example: *pobre* → *pobrecito, traje* → *trajecito*).

4. Words of one syllable ending in a consonant, attach *-ecito* or *-ecita* (for example: *pan* → *panecito*).

REPASO

I. *Escriba usted un diálogo entre una maestra y un alumno en la escuela. Trate de usar vocabulario nuevo. Escriba seis frases.*

II. *¿Cómo se dice en español?*

   1. Where are the little red blocks? _____

   _____

   2. The children are forming a set with the yellow blocks. _____

   _____

   3. This book and that one are Johnny's. My books are at home.

   _____

   4. The teacher speaks to us slowly in Spanish. _____

   _____

   5. Your house is as tall as our school. _____

   _____

   6. Little Luis only has ten pesos. He has more than I. _____

   _____

   7. Elena is the prettiest girl in the class. _____

   _____

   8. We sing more than twenty songs. _____

   _____

   9. This square is as big as that one. _____

   _____

   10. The little dog runs quickly. _____

   11. The cow is a useful animal. _____

   12. She is a good friend because she gives us milk, meat, and butter.

   _____

   13. When the cow cries, we say that she moos. _____

   _____

   14. The cow eats grass when she's hungry. _____

   _____

15. The lion is a wild animal and lives in the jungle. _____

_____

16. The dog and the horse are domestic animals. _____

_____

17. Which animals have horns on their heads? _____

_____

18. We use a knife, a fork and a spoon when we eat. _____

_____

19. We are going to see the largest animal and the smallest animal in

the zoo. _____

20. You must cross the street at the corner and wait for the light.

_____

21. She speaks as rapidly as I. _____

22. He sings as well as the teacher. _____

_____

23. Luis draws well, but Ana draws better. _____

_____

24. They have as many books as we do. _____

_____

25. Ramón is younger than Pablo, but Pepé is the youngest. _____

_____

III. _Reglas Para La Buena Salud_

¿Qué más necesita nuestro cuerpo? Nuestro cuerpo necesita alimentos especiales: estos alimentos son vitaminas. Algunas vitaminas ayudan nuestros huesos. Otras vitaminas son necesarias para tener buena vista y piel suave. Las vitaminas son necesarias para mantenernos saludables.

Las frutas tienen muchas vitaminas. Algunas frutas importantes son: las naranjas y el tomate. También tienen vitaminas los huevos, la mantequilla, la leche, el aceite de hígado, el pan, y la carne. Los vegetales frescos poseen vitaminas también.

¿Qué vitaminas hay en los alimentos que usted come cada día?

IV. *Poemas*

Sano y Fuerte

Yo quiero estar siempre,
muy sano y muy fuerte;
por eso, me tomo
buen vaso de leche;
como mantequilla,
fruta muy madura,
unos huevos tibios
y mucha verdura.

Las Frutas

Por lo menos una fruta
debes tomar cada día;
pues la fruta es muy sabrosa,
nos nutre y nos da alegría.

V. *¿Sabe usted?*

1. ¿Qué color es más claro, blanco o negro?

2. ¿Qué color es más oscuro, blanco o negro?

3. ¿Qué color usamos para colorear el tomate, el plátano, y el mar?

4. ¿Sabe usted dibujar estas formas: el cuadrado, el rectángulo, el triángulo, el círculo?

5. ¿Son más claras las noches con luna o las noches sin luna?

6. ¿Por qué la noche es oscura?

7. ¿Es redondo el círculo? ¿Sabe otra cosa redonda?

8. ¿Qué nos da la vaca?

9. ¿Dónde están las estrellas?

10. ¿Sabe usted los cinco sentidos? (La vista, el olfato, el gusto, el oído, el tacto.)

Conjugating Radical-Changing Verbs

Many verbs of the first (-*ar*) and second (-*er*) conjugations which otherwise follow a regular pattern change the radical (stem) vowels *e* to *ie* and *o* or *u* to *ue* when the stress falls on the radical vowel. In the present indicative tense, this occurs in all persons of the singular and in the third person plural. In all other forms of the verb, the stress falls on the inflectional ending and not on the stem. Therefore, there is no radical change.

Examples:

jugar (ue) - to play

yo *juego*	nosotros *jugamos*
tú *juegas*	vosotros *jugáis*
él *juega*	ella *juegan*

contar (ue) - to tell a story, to count

yo *cuento*	nosotros *contamos*
tú *cuentas*	vosotros *contáis*
él *cuenta*	ellos *cuentan*

querer (ie) - to want

yo *quiero*	nosotros *queremos*
tú *quieres*	vosotros *queréis*
él *quiere*	ellos *quieren*

poder (ue) - to be able

yo *puedo*	nosotros *podemos*
tú *puedes*	vosotros *podéis*
él *puede*	ellos *pueden*

Only third conjugation (-*ir*) verbs have a radical change in the preterite tense as well as in the present tense. In the present tense, change the stem *e* or *o* to *ie* or *i*, or *ue*, respectively. In the preterite tense (see Section XI), change the stem *e* and *o* to *i* and *u* when a diphthong begins the ending. This occurs only in the third person singular and the third person plural of the preterite tense.

Examples:

Present Tense   ### Preterite Tense

dormir (ue, u) - to sleep

yo *duermo*	nosotros *dormimos*	yo *dormí*	nosotros *dormimos*
tú *duemes*	vosotros *dormís*	tú *dormiste*	vosotros *dormisteis*
él *duerme*	ellos *duermen*	él *durmió*	ellos *durmieron*

sentir (ie,i) - to feel

yo *siento*	nosotros *sentimos*	yo *sentí*	nosotros *sentimos*
tú *sientes*	vosotros *sentís*	tú *sentiste*	vosotros *sentisteis*
él *siente*	ellos *sienten*	él *sintió*	ellos *sintieron*

pedir (i,i) - to ask for

yo *pido*	nosotros *pedimos*	yo *pedí*	nosotros *pedimos*
tú *pides*	vosotros *pedís*	tú *pediste*	vosotros *pedisteis*
él *pide*	ellos *piden*	él *pidió*	ellos *pidieron*

Some Important Radical-Changing Verbs

acostarse (ue)	to go to bed, to lie down
almorzar (ue)	to eat lunch
calentar (ie)	to heat
cerrar (ie)	to close
comenzar (ie)	to begin
contar (ue)	to count, to tell a story
despertarse (ie)	to wake up
divertirse (i,i)	to enjoy, to have a good time
dormir (ue, u)	to sleep
empezar (ie)	to begin
entender (ie)	to understand
jugar (ue)	to play
morir (ue, u)	to die
mostrar (ue)	to show
mover (ue)	to move
pedir (i,i)	to ask for, to request
perder (ie)	to lose, to ruin, to waste
poder (ue)	to be able
probar (ue)	to test, to prove, to taste
querer (ie)	to want
repetir (i,i)	to repeat
seguir (i, i)	to follow
sentarse (ie)	to sit down
sentir (ie, i)	to feel
soñar con (ue)	to dream of
vestirse (i, i)	to dress (oneself)
volar (ue)	to fly
volver (ue)	to return

Poder and *querer* are always followed by the infinitive form of the verb.

Examples:

Puedo contar.	I can sing.
Quiere comer.	He wants to eat.

REPASO

I. *¿Cómo se dice en español?*

1. Can you count the objects in the set? _____

_____

2. I want to try that game, but I am afraid. _____

_____

3. The teacher is repeating the lesson. You can understand if she speaks slowly and you listen carefully. _____

_____

4. Can you hear me? I am telling the story of <u>Red Riding Hood</u>.

_____

5. The birds fly in the sky and they return to their nest. _____

_____

6. Miss García closes the door when the class begins. _____

_____

7. The air is purer in the country and less pure in the city.

_____

8. Humans and plants cannot live without water. _____

_____

9. Water has many forms. There is water in the sea, in the river, in the lake, and in the pond. _____

_____

10. A magnet attracts things made of iron, because it has a special force. _____

_____

11. The sun gives us light and warmth. _____

_____

12. Plants need the light and warmth of the sun. _____

_____

13. The sun rises in the east, and in the morning hours it is very low and the shadows are large. _____

_____

14. At noon the sun is very high and the shadows are short. _____

   _____

15. When the weather changes, our clothes change. _____

   _____

II. *Escriba usted sus propias frases usando los verbos nuevos y algunas palabras nuevas también. Trate usted de usar frases importantes de la clase.*

III. *Canción*

Martinillo
(Tune: Are You Sleeping, Brother John)

Martinillo, Martinillo,
¿Duermes ya? ¿Duermes ya?
Toca las campanas, toca las
* campanas,*
din, don, dan, din, don, dan.

La Cucaracha

La cucaracha, la cucaracha,
ya no puede caminar,
porque no tiene, porque le falta
limonada para tomar.

IV. *Poema*

Dos pajaritos

Dos pajaritos muy sentados
En un árbol muy alto.
Vuela Panchito, vuela Pedrito,
Vuelve Pancho, vuelve Pedrito.

V. *Juego*

La Vieja Inés

(Para practicar los colores y las formas de querer.)

Choose one child to be "*la vieja Inés*," another "*la madre*," and the others "*sus niños*." Each child takes the name of a color. Place the children behind the mother. Draw a large circle on the ground some distance away. "*La vieja Inés*" faces "*la madre*" and pretends to knock on a door and says,

Tan, tan
Madre: *¿Quién es?*
Inés: *La vieja Inés.*
Madre: *¿Qué quieres?*
Inés: *Quiero colores.*
Madre: *¿Qué color quieres?*
Inés: *Quiero rojo* (or any color).

The "*niño*" who is "*rojo*" runs, followed by Inés and tries to reach home base before being caught. If he succeeds, he returns to his place behind "*la madre*." Game continues until all the colors have been chosen. The last one caught becomes "*la madre*" and another "*Inés*" is chosen.

VI. *Historia*

El Año Nuevo

Este día es de regocijo en México. Todas las familias tienen como costumbre el de reunirse (padres, hermanos, cuañados, primos, sobrinos, etc.) para así recibir al año nuevo.

Cuando entra el año nuevo se acostumbra a disparar cohetes y pistolas. Las campanas de las iglesias también empiezan a tocar. El primero de enero las familias van a visitar a parientes y amigos para "dar el año nuevo," o sea, desear felicidad y prosperidad en el año que acaba de comenzar.

Algunos de los platillos que se sirven en ciertas partes de México (como el sur de México) son tamales, buñuelos, y capirotada.

Reflexive Verbs

The verb is reflexive when the subject and the object pronoun are the same person or thing, that is, when the subject does something to, or acts upon itself. To make a verb reflexive, use the following reflexive pronouns:

me	myself	nos	ourselves
te	yourself (familiar)	os	yourselves (familiar plural)
se	himself, herself	se	themselves
se	yourself (polite singular)	se	yourselves (polite plural)

Reflexive pronouns follow the same position rules as direct and indirect object pronouns. They are attached to the infinitive, the affirmative commands, and the present participle and precede a negative command. In the dictionary, reflexive verbs have the third person reflexive pronoun attached to the infinitive.

Reflexive pronouns do not alter the original verb form; therefore, all reflexive verbs follow the model given here:

llamarse - to be called; to be named

yo me llamo	I call myself, I am named
tú te llamas	You call yourself, you are named
él se llama	He calls himself, he is named
ella se llama	She calls herself, she is named
usted se llama	You call yourself, you are named
nosotros (-as) nos llamamos	We call ourselves, we are named
vosotros os llamáis	You call yourselves, you are named
ellos se llaman	They call themselves, they are named
ellas se llaman	They call themselves, they are named
ustedes se llaman	You call yourselves, you are named

Examples:

¿Cómo te llamas?	What's your name?
Me llamo Rosa.	My name is Rosa (I call myself Rosa).

Verbs are reflexive only if the subject acts upon itself, not if the subject acts upon something else.

Examples:

Me lavo las manos.	I wash my hands. (reflexive)
Yo lavo la ropa.	I wash the clothes. (not reflexive)
El se levanta.	He gets up. (reflexive)
Su mamá le levanta.	His mother gets him up. (not reflexive)
El niño se esconde allí.	The child hides there. (reflexive)
El niño esconde el dulce allí.	The child hides the candy there. (not reflexive)

Many verbs that are reflexive in Spanish are not reflexive in English, and consequently do not make sense translated to English. The only way to approach these verbs is to memorize them. Following is a list of important reflexive verbs:

acordarse de (ue)	to remember
acostarse (ue)	to go to bed, to lie down
bañarse	to take a bath
caerse	to fall down
callarse	to be quiet
cansarse	to get tired
casarse con	to marry
cepillarse	to brush
desayunarse	to eat breakfast
desvestirse (i, i)	to get undressed
dormirse (ue, u)	to fall asleep
enfadarse	to get angry
enojarse	to get angry
esconderse	to hide
hacerse	to become something (plus noun)
irse	to go away
lavarse	to wash (oneself)
levantarse	to get up
limpiarse	to clean
llamarse	to be called, to be named
marcharse	to go away
mejorarse	to get better
pararse	to stand up, to stop
peinarse	to comb one's hair
ponerse	to put on (clothing), to become (plus adjective)
quedarse	to stay, to remain
quitarse	to take off (clothing)
sentarse (ie)	to sit down
subirse	to climb up
vestirse (i, i)	to get dressed

Polite Commands

Formation: Use the stem of the <u>first person singular</u> of the <u>present indicative tense</u> to form the polite (or formal) command of regular verbs, irregular verbs, and radical changing verbs. Verbs ending in -ar, add -e (singular) and -en (plural). Verbs ending in -er or -ir, add -a (singular) and -an (plural). Although in English we do not distinguish singular and plural commands, we do in Spanish.

	<u>Infinitive</u>	Present Tense First Person <u>Singular</u>	<u>Stem</u>
Regular	*ayudar*	*ayudo*	*ayud-*
	beber	*bebo*	*beb-*
	vivir	*vivo*	*viv-*
Irregular	*tener*	*tengo*	*teng-*
	decir	*digo*	*dig-*
Rad. Chg.	*jugar*	*juego*	*jueg-*
	cerrar	*cierro*	*cierr-*

Command

<u>Singular</u>	<u>Plural</u>
ayude Ud.	*ayuden Uds.*
beba Ud.	*beban Uds.*
viva Ud.	*vivan Uds.*
tenga Ud.	*tengan Uds.*
diga Ud.	*digan Uds.*
juege Ud.	*juegen Uds.*
cierre Ud.	*cierren Uds.*

The subject of the command, *Ud.* or *Uds.*, may be omitted. Use *no* before the affirmative command to state a polite negative command.

Examples:

Abra la puerta.	<u>Open the door.</u>
No abra la puerta.	<u>Don't open the door.</u>
Cierre (Ud.) la puerta, *por favor.*	<u>Please close the door.</u>
¡Tengan Ud. cuidado!	<u>Be careful!</u>
Tome Ud. el agua.	<u>Drink the water.</u>

Attach object pronouns--direct object, indirect object, or both--to affirmative commands and put them immediately preceding negative commands. When combining a multisyllabic command with an object pronoun, use an accent mark to indicate the original stress of the command.

Examples:

Lléveselo Ud. a él.	Take it to him.
No se lo lleve Ud.	Don't take it to him.
Tómela ahora.	Drink it now.
No la tome ahora.	Don't drink it now.
Dígamelo.	Tell me it.
No me lo diga.	Don't tell me it.

Irregular Polite Commands

The following verbs do not follow the above rules for polite command formation and should be memorized.

		Singular	Plural
estar	to be	*esté Ud.*	*estén Uds.*
dar	to give	*dé Ud.*	*den Uds.*
ir	to go	*vaya Ud.*	*vayan Uds.*
ser	to be	*sea Ud.*	*sean Uds.*
saber	to know	*sepa Ud.*	*sepan Uds.*

Usage of Informal Commands

Spanish has two sets of commands: polite or formal (*usted*) commands and familiar or informal (*tú*) commands. The polite or formal commands, just listed, are used by people who address others as *Ud.* or *Uds.* The informal commands are used by people who address others as *tú* or *vosotros*. Because *ustedes* functions as the plural of *tú* in Spanish American, the plural formal command corresponding to *ustedes* is also used as the plural informal command.

To form the informal or familiar (*tú*) command, simply use the <u>third person singular</u> of the <u>present indicative</u>.

Present Indicative	Affirmative *tú* Command
él habla	*habla tú*

To form the singular negative *tú* command, use the polite (*usted*) command +*s:*

Polite (*usted*) Command	Negative Informal (*tú*) Command
hable usted	*no hables tú*

For the plural of the *tú* or informal command in Spanish American, the polite (plural) command is used: *hablen ustedes.*

As with the formal commands, there are some verbs which are irregular in the informal command and must be learned:

Affirmative

poner	*pon*
tener	*ten*
salir	*sal*
venir	*ven*
hacer	*haz*
decir	*di*
ser	*sé*
ir	*ve*

For the plural of these irregular verbs, use the polite plural (*pongan, salgan,* etc.). For the negative, we follow the same rule as the regular informal commands. Use the polite command *+s*.

Examples:

¡Sal! (tú)	Leave! (informal)
¡Salga usted!	Leave! (formal)
No salgas (tú).	Don't leave. (informal)

Summary

	Polite	Informal
hablar		
singular	*hable usted*	*habla tú*
plural	*hablen ustedes*	*hablen*
negative	*no hable usted*	*no hables*
	no hablen ustedes	*no hablen*
decir		
singular	*diga usted*	*di tú*
plural	*digan ustedes*	*digan*
negative	*no diga usted*	*no digas*
	no digan ustedes	*no digan*

Favor De Plus an Infinitive

An acceptable substitute for the polite command is *favor de* plus an infinitive. Translate it as please do something.

Examples:

Favor de darme el lápiz.	Please give me the pencil.
Favor de no hablar por un minuto.	Please do not speak for one minute.

Some Helpful Commands in the Class

Below are some commonly used classroom expressions. These expressions must be adjusted according to your group. They are all given in the familiar or informal, singular command form. If working with young children, common usage dictates that the teacher address the children using the *tú* form, or the informal command. However, if addressing older students, the *usted* form might be appropriate.

¡Entra! ¡Pasa!	Come in!
Silencio.	Quiet.
Tráeme . . .	Bring me . . .
Ven acá.	Come here.
¡Atención!	Attention!
Ten cuidado.	Be careful.
Dispénsame.	Excuse me.
Por favor.	Please.
Perdóname.	Pardon me.
Está bien.	O.K.
Léelo en voz alta.	Read it aloud.
Siéntate.	Sit down.
Repite, por favor.	Repeat, please.
Cierra el libro.	Close the book.
Abre su libro.	Open your book.
Contesta.	Answer.
Empieza.	Begin.
Obedece las instrucciones.	Follow the directions.
Escucha bien.	Listen carefully.
Levanta la mano.	Raise your hand.
¡Mira!	Look!
Habla más alto, por favor.	Speak louder, please.
Ponte . . .	Put on . . .
Quítate . . .	Take off . . .
¿Me oyes?	Do you hear me?
Practica.	Practice.
Corrige.	Correct.
Vuelve a sentarte.	Take your seat.
Sigue leyendo.	Go on reading.
Pronuncia con cuidado.	Pronounce carefully.
Pasa al pizarrón.	Go to the blackboard.
No hables tan de prisa.	Don't speak so fast.

REPASO

I. *¿Cómo se dice en español?*

1. The bull defends himself with his horns. _____

   _____

2. Some animals feed on other animals. _____

   _____

3. It is important to brush your teeth and wash your hands. _____

   _____

4. Wait for the traffic light and be careful, Juanito. _____

   _____

5. Please close the door and sit down._____

   _____

6. The children hide in the garden. _____

   _____

7. Take a bath every day and put on clean clothes. _____

   _____

8. Do it now and don't tell me that you cannot. _____

   _____

9. Hi! What's your name? _____

10. Some flowers turn into fruits. _____

    _____

11. Color the picture and put it on the bulletin board, Juanita.

    _____

12. Please don't leave now, friends, wait for the bus. _____

    _____

13. If you don't understand the lesson, tell me. _____

    _____

14. Go to the store, buy a small bread, and return home quickly, Pedro. _____

15. Come in, Mrs. García, and sit down. _____

_____

16. Don't speak to me that way! Be quiet! _____

_____

17. Open your books and read ten pages. _____

_____

18. The children are putting on their coats. _____

_____

19. Go away now and come back later. _____

_____

20. Count the blocks and make a square with the red blocks. _____

_____

II. *Canciones*

Saludable
(Tune: Mulberry Bush)

Esto es todo lo que debo hacer
Que debo hacer, que debo hacer;
Esto es todo lo que debo hacer,
Para estar saludable.

Así la cara me lavo yo,
Me lavo yo, me lavo yo,
Así la cara me lavo yo,
Temprano por la mañana.

Así los dientes me cepillo,
Me cepillo, me cepillo;
Así los dientes me cepillo,
Temprano por la mañana.

Así el cabello me peino yo,
Me peino yo, me peino yo,
Así el cabello me peino yo,
Temprano por la mañana.

Así las uñas me limpio yo,
Me limpio yo, me limpio yo,
Así las uñas me limpio yo,
Temprano por la mañana.

(Tune: Open Shut Them)

Ábranlas, ciérrenlas
Ábranlas, ciérrenlas
Pla-pla-pla-pla-pla.

Ábranlas, ciérrenlas
Ábranlas, ciérrenlas
Ponganlas acá.

Cielito Lindo

De la Sierra Morena,
Cielito lindo
vienen bajando,
un par de ojitos negros,
Cielito lindo
de contrabando.

Ay, ay, ay, ay,
Canta y no llores;
Porque cantando se alegran,
Cielito lindo
los corazones.

III. Poema

Las Estaciones

¿Cómo te llamas, hermosa niña?
Me llamo Primavera.
Yo traigo los pájaros y las flores.
Cuando llego los árboles se cubren de hojas
nuevas y el labrador echa la semilla en el surco.

¿Quién eres tú?
Soy el Verano.
Conmigo viene el calor.
Cuando llego los pájaros cantan en sus nidos
y las abejas hacen su panal.

¿Cómo te llamas, niño?
Mi nombre es Otoño.
A mí me acompañan siempre las nubes y la lluvia.
Yo pinto los árboles y los campos de color de oro.

¿Quién eres tú, niño?
Soy el Invierno.
Cuando llego los pajaritos se van.
Los niños se ponen sus abrigos y no salen a jugar.
Yo quito las hojas secas de los árboles para que cubran
las pequeñas plantas.

IV. Adivinanzas

El semáforo

Tengo un ojo verde
y otro rojo.
Con el rojo te paras
con el verde
caminas.

A E I O U

A E I O U
Arbolito de Pirú
Yo me llamo _____
 Cómo te llamas tú?

El Espejo

Te acercas a él
y en él te ves,
¿Qué es?

Mis Ojos

Mis ojos, mis ojos
Se cierran y se abren,
Mis ojos, mis ojos,
Se cierran así.

Mi boca, mi boca
Se cierra y se abre
Mis manos, mis manos,
Se cierran así.

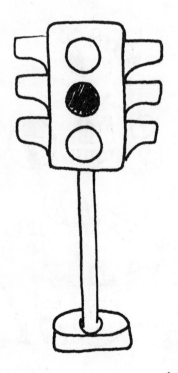

Present Participles

To form the present participle of a verb, drop the infinitive ending and add *-ando* to the stem of *-ar* verbs and *-iendo* to the stem of *-er* and *-ir* verbs. The English present participle ends in -ing.

Examples:

ayudar:	*ayud*	*ando*	=	*ayudando*	helping
beber:	*beb*	*iendo*	=	*bebiendo*	drinking
sufrir:	*sufr*	*iendo*	=	*sufriendo*	suffering

A few verbs have irregularities in the present participle. The *i* of *-iendo* becomes *y* between vowels:

Examples:

leer	→	*leyendo*	reading
creer	→	*creyendo*	believing

In stem changing *-ir* verbs, whose stem vowel changes *o* to *u* or *e* to *i* in the third person preterite, the same change occurs in the present participle.

Examples:

decir:	*diciendo*	saying, telling
mentir:	*mintiendo*	lying
pedir:	*pidiendo*	asking for
morir:	*muriendo*	dying
seguir:	*siguiendo*	following, continuing
ir:	*yendo*	going
dormir:	*durmiendo*	sleeping

Progressive Action (Present Progressive Tense)

Both Spanish and English have present progressive tenses which are similarly formed and used. Progressive action is a word-for-word translation of the verb. Use the present progressive tense for an action in progress. Most uses of the progressive tense in Spanish emphasize what is happening at that moment. Use the present tense of the verb *estar* before the present participle of a verb to express progressive action in the present tense.

Examples:

estar aprendiendo	to be learning
Estoy aprendiendo.	I am learning.
Estás aprendiendo.	You are learning.
Está aprendiendo.	He is learning.
Estamos aprendiendo.	We are learning.
Estáis aprendiendo.	You are learning.
Están aprendiendo.	They, you (pl) are learning.

Note that the present participle is the same for all persons and all tenses. Only the conjugation of *estar* changes to agree with the subject.

Examples:

Ella está tomando agua.	She is drinking water.
Están comiendo.	They are eating.
Está durmiendo.	She is sleeping.
¿Está Ud. estudiando mucho?	Are you studying a lot?
El niño está escribiendo la lección.	The boy is writing the lesson.

Direct, indirect and reflexive pronouns may either precede the conjugated verb form of *estar* or be attached to the present participle. An accent mark is required on the stressed vowel of the present participle when one or more pronouns are attached to it.

Example:

Está escribiéndolo.	He is writing it.
Lo está escribiendo.	

Past Participles

To form the past participle, add *-ado* to an *-ar* verb stem, and *-ido* to *-er* and *-ir* verb stems.

Examples:

terminar:	*termin*	*ado*	=	*terminado*	finished
comprender:	*comprend*	*ido*	=	*comprendido*	understood
unir:	*un*	*ido*	=	*unido*	united, connected

Verbs having other endings are irregular, generally because they keep the Latin form of the participle. You will find these irregular past participles useful to know.

abrir:	*abierto*	opened
cubrir:	*cubierto*	covered
decir:	*dicho*	said
escribir:	*escrito*	written

hacer:	*hecho*	done
morir:	*muerto*	dead
poner:	*puesto*	put, placed
romper:	*roto*	broken
ver:	*visto*	seen
volver:	*vuelto*	turned, returned

Use the past participle to form adjectives from verbs. As adjectives, they must agree in number and gender with the noun they modify.

Examples:

(cansar: cansado)
El caballo está cansado.   The horse is tired.

(morir: muerto)
La mosca está muerta.   The fly is dead.

(romper: roto)
El lápiz está roto.   The pencil is broken.

The past participle with *haber* is also used to form the perfect tenses.

REPASO

I.   *¡Escriba usted las formas correctas de los infinitivos en la lista!*

		Present Participle	Past Participle
1.	*dibujar*	_____	_____
2.	*comprender*	_____	_____
3.	*ver*	_____	_____
4.	*volver*	_____	_____
5.	*poner*	_____	_____
6.	*hacer*	_____	_____
7.	*lavar*	_____	_____
8.	*correr*	_____	_____
9.	*cubrir*	_____	_____
10.	*meter*	_____	_____

	Present Participle	Past Participle
11. *viajar*	_____	_____
12. *colorar*	_____	_____
13. *contar*	_____	_____
14. *esconder*	_____	_____
15. *leer*	_____	_____

II. *¿Cómo se dice en español?*

1. The teacher is reading us a story and we are listening to it.

_____

2. We are learning to speak English and our friends are learning to speak Spanish. _____

_____

3. The drawing is finished. Do you want to see it? _____

_____

4. They are counting the blocks. One block is broken and the teacher is putting it in the wastebasket. _____

_____

5. We are playing and running and singing. _____

_____

6. What are you doing now? I'm watching T.V. _____

_____

7. She is writing it on the blackboard. _____

_____

8. The sun is shining and the cows are sleeping in the grass. _____

_____

9. I'm looking for the book in the library. _____

_____

10. She is eating with her friends in the cafeteria. _____

_____

III. *Un drama*

Doña Zorra Y Doña Cigüeña

Doña Zorra prepara un banquete. La mesa está puesta para dos. En la mesa hay dos platos anchos de fina porcelana. El caldo de pollo está pre-parado. Doña Zorro se pone su mejor piel. Da los últimos toques a su peinado. Llama a la puerta. Es Doña Cigüeña.

--¡Qué elegante estás, chica!-- dice Doña Zorra.

--Hoy llevo mis mejores plumas blancas. Además, acabo de afilarme el pico porque tengo mucha hambre.

--¡A la mesa, pues!

Se sientan Doña Zorra y Doña Cigüeña. Empiezan a comer. Doña Cigüeña picotea y picotea y no alcanza nada. Doña Zorra lame y lame y limpia el plato. Doña Cigüeña se desespera. Picotea otra vez. Se levanta. Se sienta otra vez. Picotea y no consigue nada. Por fin, sale muerta de hambre. Doña Zorra se lame el otro plato, también.

Pasa una semana. Doña Cigüeña preparea un banquete. La mesa está puesta para dos, también. En la mesa no hay platos. Hay dos vasos altos de fina porcelana. El caldo de pescado está preparado. Doña Cigüeña se pone sus mejores plumas. Tiene su pico bien afilado. Llama a la puerta. Es Doña Zorra.

--¡Qué elegante estás, chica !-- dice Doña Cigüeña.

--Hoy llevo mi mejor piel. Además, acabo de peinarme. Tengo mucha hambre.

--¡A la mesa, pues!

Se sientan Doña Cigüeña y Doña Zorra. Empiezan a comer. Doña Zorra lame y lame y no alcanza nada. El vaso es demasiado alto y estrecho para su hocico. Doña Cigüeña picotea y picotea y limpia su plato. Se ríe. Doña Zorra se desespera. Lame otra vez. Se levanta. Lame y no consigue nada. Se sienta otra vez. Doña Cigüeña se ríe. Doña Zorra se levanta. Coge su piel y se va. Doña Cigüeña se ríe con más ganas.

--¿Por qué te ríes, pico largo?-- dice Doña Zorra.

--Me río porque te quedas con hambre.

Doña Zorra, enfadada, sale con la cola despeinada entre sus patas.

Doña Cigüeña le grita --También hay engaños para pícaros. ¡Adiós, chica!

Vocabulario

picotear	-	to peck, to nibble
zorra	-	fox
cigüeña	-	stork
afilarse	-	sharpen
lamer	-	to lick
reírse	-	to laugh

¿Puede usted explicar el cuento en sus propias palabras?

¿Puede usted ilustrar la misma idea de otra manera?

Forming the Preterite Tense

To form the preterite tense, add the following endings to the stem of the verb:

-é, -aste, -ó, -amos, -asteis, and -aron to first conjugation -ar verbs;

-í, -iste, -ió, -imos, -isteis, and -ieron to second conjugation -er verbs;

-í, -iste, -ió, -imos, -isteis, and -ieron to third conjugation -ir verbs.

Examples:

cantar (stem: cant-)

canté	I sang, I did sing
cantaste	You sang, you did sing
cantó	He, she, you sang, did sing
cantamos	We sang, we did sing
cantasteis	You sang, you did sing
cantaron	They, you (pl.) sang, did sing

aprender (stem: aprend-)

aprendí	I learned, I did learn
aprendiste	You learned, you did learn
aprendió	He, she, you learned, did learn
aprendimos	We learned, we did learn
aprendisteis	You learned, you did learn
aprendieron	They, you (pl.) learned, did learn

escriber (stem: escrib-)

escribí	I wrote, I did write
escribiste	You wrote, you did write
escribió	He, she, you wrote, did write
escribimos	We wrote, we did write
escribisteis	You wrote, you did write
escribieron	They, you (pl.) wrote, did write

Using the Preterite Tense

Use the preterite tense when an action or state in the past is definitely completed, or limited. Did plus the meaning of the verb is one of the key words in the translation of this tense.

Examples:

¿Dónde vivió usted el año pasado?	Where did you live last year?
No canté hoy.	I didn't sing today.
¿Cuándo nació?	When were you born?
¿Qué pasó?	What happened?

Irregular Preterite Tense Verbs

dar	to give	*dí, diste, dió, dimos, disteis, dieron*
decir	to say, to tell	*dije, dijiste, dijo, dijimos, dijisteis, dijeron*
estar	to be	*estuve, estuviste, estuvo, estuvimos, estuvisteis, estuvieron*
haber	to have	*hube, hubiste, hubo, hubimos, hubisteis, hubieron*
ir, ser	to go, to be	*fuí, fuiste, fué, fuimos, fuisteis, fueron*
poder	to be able	*pude, pudiste, pudo, pudimos, pudisteis, pudieron*
poner	to put, to place	*puse, pusiste, puso, pusimos, pusisteis, pusieron*
querer	to want	*quise, quisiste, quiso, quisimos, quisisteis, quisieron*
tener	to have	*tuve, tuviste, tuvo, tuvimos, tuvisteis, tuvieron*
venir	to come	*vine, viniste, vino, vinimos, vinisteis, vinie...*
ver	to see	*ví, viste, vió, vimos, visteis, vieron*

With certain verbs like *leer, oír, creer, caer,* and *construir,* the third person singular ends in *-yó* and the third person plural ends in *-yeron.* An unaccented *i* can never stand between vowels. The remaining forms have a written accent mark over the *i* to show that a diphthong is not formed in speaking.

Example:

leer

leí	*leímos*
leíste	*leísteis*
leyó	*leyeron*

Stem-changing verbs with *-ir* endings change the stem in the third person singular and the third person plural in the preterite tense. (See page 85, Section VIII on Radical-Changing Verbs for a review of this.)

Examples:

El puso los bloques en la mesa.	He put the blocks on the table.

La niña no pidió nada.	<u>The little girl didn't ask for anything</u>.
Ella se vistió.	<u>She got dressed</u>.
El no dijo nada.	<u>He didn't say anything</u>.
No oí la canción.	<u>I didn't hear the song</u>.
Ellos durmieron en la clase.	<u>They slept in the class</u>.

In Spanish, use a double negative, that is, put *no* before the verb and a negative word following the verb, as in some of the examples above.

REPASO

I. *Conteste usted las preguntas <u>en español</u>.*

1. *¿Cómo te llamas?* _____

2. *¿Qué hora es?* _____

3. *¿Cuántos años tienes?* _____

4. *¿De dónde eres?* _____

5. *¿Qué estás leyendo?* _____

6. *¿Dónde naciste?* _____

7. *¿Dónde está tu casita?* _____

8. *¿Qué comiste esta mañana?* _____

9. *¿A qué hora te acostaste anoche?* _____

10. *¿A qué hora te levantaste esta mañana?* _____

11. *¿Comprendes mejor cuando leo en inglés o en español?* _____

    _____

12. *¿Quién te leyó el cuento de <u>Los Tres Osos</u>?* _____

    _____

13. *¿A dónde fuiste ayer?* _____

14. *¿Dónde pusiste tus creyones?* _____

15. *¿Qué hiciste con estos colores?* _____

II. *¿Cómo se dice en español?*

1. What book did you read yesterday? _____

_____

2. Where did you learn to speak English? _____

_____

3. They didn't say anything but they listened carefully. _____

_____

4. The girl got dressed and ran to school. _____

_____

5. Ana didn't hear the sound of the letter <u>j</u>. _____

_____

6. They sang the song and the teacher played the guitar. _____

_____

7. We saw you yesterday and gave you the crayons. _____

_____

8. They built a beautiful building with the blocks, but it fell down.

_____

9. What did the teacher say when you gave her the tortillas? _____

_____

10. Please sit down and study the lesson. _____

_____

11. Did you see the cat? He is hiding in the grass. _____

_____

12. He didn't give the candy to his friends. He ate it all! _____

_____

13. You may play and run, but do not push! _____

_____

14. Tell me everything about your family. _____

_____

15. Do you have (any) brothers and sisters? _____

_____

16. What is today's date? _____

17. Where did the teacher go? _____

18. The class went to the library. _____

_____

19. What did you see in the zoo? _____

_____

20. I saw many animals and I gave them food. _____

_____

III. *Poemas*

Primavera

Ya llegó la primavera entre pájaros y flores;
trae a la oreja prendidos, aretillos de colores.
Guarda en las manos niditos de jilgueros y verdines;
y trae un manto formado de azucenas y jazmines.
Ya llegó la primavera entre nubes de ilusión;
*   porque de amor y de dicha, es su mágica misión.*

El Osito

Mira este osito,
que bonito está;
me lo dieron anoche
mi mamá y mi papá.

El Columpio

Muy alto subí
pero me caí
Gritando me fuí
i - i - i - i

Los Meses Del Año

Primer mes del año
Enero ya llegó,
primer mes del año,
primer . . . año,
y enero y salió.

Segundo mes del año
En el mes de febrero,
blanca nieve cayó,
nieve . . . cayó,
febrero ya acabó.

Tercer mes del año
Marzo aquí volvió,
fuerte el viento sopló,
viento . . . sopló,
y marzo terminó.

Cuarto mes del año
El mes de abril llegó,
la lluvia empezó,
lluvia . . . empezó,
y el mes de abril salió.

Quinto mes del año
Mayo floreció,
y el pasto ya creció,
pasto . . . creció,
y mayo terminó.

Sexto mes del año
Junio ya llegó,
sexto mes del año,
sexto . . . año,
y junio ya salió.

Séptimo mes del año
En el mes de julio,
el cucú ya cantó,
cucú . . . cantó,
y julio ya acabó.

Octavo mes del año
Agosto ya empezó,
y el calor ya subió,
calor . . . subió,
y agosto ya salió.

Noveno mes del año
Septiembre regresó,
la escuela ya se abrió,
escuela . . . abrió,
septiembre ya acabó.

Décimo mes del año
Octubre ya llegó,
el otoño empezó,
otoño . . . empezó,
y octubre terminó.

Onceavo mes del año
Noviembre empezó,
y el cielo gris cubrió,
cielo . . . cubrió,
noviembre se acabó.

Doceavo mes del año
Diciembre ya volvió,
último del año,
último . . . año,
y el año terminó.

¡FELIZ AÑO NUEVO!

Recoger Fruta

La manzana se cayó
y la quise comer yo.
Pero, lástima me dió
al gritarme - o-o-o-o

IV. *Canción*

La Pequeñita Araña
(Tune: Eency Weency Spider)

La pequeñita araña
subía por la manga.
Vino la lluvia
y se la llevó
Salió el sol
y todo lo secó
y la pequeñita araña
subió y subió y subió.

V. *Cuento con moraleja*

El Zorro y La Corneja

Una vez un zorro vió a una corneja con un pedazo de queso en el pico.
La corneja se detuvo en la rama de un árbol. El zorro pensó: --Yo quiero
ese pedazo de queso.-- Entonces se acercó al árbol y le dijo a la corneja:
--Buenos días, Señorita Corneja, ¡Qué brillantes ojos tiene! Estoy seguro
que su voz es más bonita que la de los pájaros.

La corneja levantó la cabeza y comenzó a cantar horriblemente. Al
momento que abrió el pico, se cayó el queso al suelo. El zorro pronto
levantó el pedazo de queso y le dijo a la corneja: --Esto era lo que yo
quería. . . En cambio por el pedazo de queso, le doy este consejo. ¡No
se crea de lisonjeros!

VI. *Un drama*

Los Tres Osos

Había una vez tres osos: un oso grande, el papá; un oso mediano, la
mamá; y un oso pequeño, el niño. Los tres osos viven en una casa en un
bosque.

En la casa de los tres osos hay tres camas; una cama grande para el
oso grande, una cama mediana para el oso mediano, una cama pequeña para
el oso pequeño.

En la casa hay también tres sillas: una silla grande, una silla
mediana y una silla pequeña para el oso pequeño.

En la casa hay también una mesa. En la mesa hay tres platos; un
plato grande, un plato mediano y un plato pequeño para el oso pequeño.

En la mesa hay tres cucharas: una cuchara grande, una cuchara
mediana, y una cuchara pequeña para el oso pequeño.

Un día el oso grande dice: --Tengo hambre.

El oso mediano dice, --Yo tengo mucha hambre.

Y el oso pequeño repite, --Yo tengo mucha hambre también.

La mamá prepara la comida. Prepara una sopa rica y sabrosa. El oso grande toma la cuchara grande, prueba la sopa y dice, --La sopa está caliente.

El oso mediano toma la cuchara mediana, prueba la sopa y dice, --Sí, la sopa está muy caliente.

El oso pequeño toma la cuchara pequeña, prueba la sopa y dice, --Sí, sí, la sopa está muy caliente.

El oso grande dice, --Vamos a dar un paseo por el bosque. Vamos a tomar la sopa más tarde.

Los tres osos van al bosque. Dejan la puerta de la casa abierta. Una niña entra en la casa de los tres osos.

--Mmmmm. . . ¡Qué sopa tan rica! Tengo hambre,-- dice la niña.

Toma la cuchara grande, prueba la sopa que hay en el plato grande y dice, --¡Esta sopa está muy caliente!

Entonces toma la cuchara mediana, prueba la sopa que hay en el plato mediano y dice, -- Esta sopa está muy caliente también.

Entonces toma la cuchara pequeña y prueba la sopa que hay en el plato pequeño y dice, --¡Esta sopa es muy buena!-- y se toma toda la sopa que hay en el plato del oso pequeño . . .

La niña ve las tres sillas. Está muy cansada. Se sienta en la silla grande y dice, --Esta silla no es cómoda.

Se sienta en la silla mediana y dice, --Esta silla no es cómoda.

Entonces se sienta en la silla pequeña y dice, --Esta silla es muy cómoda.

Pero la silla es muy pequeña y se rompe.

La niña dice entonces, --Tengo sueño.

Se acuesta en la cama grande y dice, --Esta cama no es cómoda.

Se acuesta en la cama mediana y dice, --Esta cama no es cómoda.

Se acuesta en la cama pequeña y dice, --Esta cama es muy cómoda,-- y la niña se duerme.

Un momento después los osos entran en la casa.

El oso grande ve su cuchara y su plato y dice, --Alguien entró aquí y probó mi sopa.

El oso mediano ve su cuchara y su plato y dice, --Sí, alguien entró aquí y probó mi sopa también.

El oso pequeño ve su cuchara y su plato y dice, --Sí, sí, alguien entró aquí y se tomó toda mi sopa.

Entonces el oso grande ve su silla y dice, --Alguien entró aquí y se sentó en mi silla,--y el oso pequeño dice, --Sí, sí, alguien entró aquí y rompió mi silla.

El oso pequeño llora.

Entonces el oso grande ve su cama y dice, --Alguien entró aquí y se acostó en mi cama.

El oso pequeño ve su cama y dice, --Sí, sí. ¡Mamá! ¡Papá! Hay una niña en mi cama.

Los tres osos van a la cama del oso pequeño.

En este momento la niña abre los ojos, ve a los tres osos y grita, --¡Ay! ¡Tengo miedo!

La niña se levanta de la cama, sale y corre, corre por el bosque.

1. ¿Puede usted explicar el cuento en sus propias palabras (en español)?

2. ¿Puede usted ilustrar el cuento con objetos de la casa o ilustraciones?

SECTION XII

Hay Idiomatically

Use *hay* to express the impersonal <u>there is</u>, <u>there are</u>, <u>is there</u>, and <u>are there</u>.

Examples:

No hay nadie en el cuarto.	<u>There is nobody in the room.</u>
Hay muchos estudiantes en la escuela.	<u>There are many students in the school</u>.
¿Hay preguntas?	<u>Are there any questions?</u>
Si hay algún problema, avíseme.	<u>If there is any problem, call me.</u>

Use the imperfect singular form of *haber (había)* to express <u>there was</u>, <u>there were</u>, <u>was there</u>, and <u>were there</u>.

Examples:

Había muchos bloques en la caja.	<u>There were many blocks in the box.</u>
¿Había muchos libros en la biblioteca?	<u>Were there many books in the library</u>.

The Preposition A

An important difference between English and Spanish sentences is the Spanish use of the preposition *a* to introduce a direct object noun referring to a definite person or persons.

Example:

María lleva a los niños a la escuela.	<u>Maria is taking the children to school</u>

If a direct object noun refers to persons in general, rather than to a definite person or persons, do not use the preposition *a*.

Example:

María lleva niños a la escuela.	<u>Maria takes children to school.</u>

If the direct object noun does not refer to persons, do not use *a*.

Example:

María lleva los libros a la biblioteca.	Maria is taking the books to the library.

Acabar De (To Have Just)

Use *acabar de* before an infinitive to express an action completed in the immediate past or an action in conjunction with another event. The time expressed depends upon the tense used. The present tense of *acabar de* expresses an action <u>just</u> completed; the imperfect tense of *acabar de* denotes a past action completed in conjunction with another event.

Examples:

La maestra acaba de llegar.	The teacher has just arrived.
Acabo de leer el libro.	I have just read the book.
Los niños acaban de terminar la lección.	The children have just finished the lesson.
Acabamos de oír el cuento.	We have just heard the story.
Acababa de hablar inglés cuando salió de la escuela.	He had just learned to speak English when he left the school.

REPASO

I. *¿Cómo se dice en español?*

1. The children have just arrived at school. _____

   _____

2. I have just seen the new teacher. _____

   _____

3. Is there any more chalk in the classroom? _____

   _____

4. The teacher takes the little boy to the bathroom. _____

   _____

5. There are many students in the class and there aren't enough chairs.

   _____

6. I have just gone to visit John. _____

_____

7. There aren't any other relatives in this part of the city. _____

_____

8. The mother took her children to the bakery. _____

_____

9. They have just had an ice cream. _____

_____

10. Are there any questions? _____

Interrogative Words

Use *cuál (es)* (which) to refer to person or things when choosing one of more from a larger group.

Examples:

¿*Cuál de los colores es azul?*	Which (one) of the colors is blue?
¿*Cuáles de las maestras son simpáticas?*	Which (ones) of the teachers are nice?
¿*Cuál es su hermano?*	Which (one) is your brother?
¿*Cuáles son sus hermanos?*	Which (ones) are your brothers?

Use *cuál* (what) preceding *ser*. Use *qué* when requesting an explanation.

Examples:

¿*Cuál es la fecha (de hoy)?*	What is the date?
¿*Cuál es su ocupación?*	What is your occupation?
¿*Cuál es su nacionalidad?*	What is your nationality?
¿*Qué es esto?*	What is this? (explanation)

In all other cases, except idioms, use *qué* to express what.

Examples:

¿*Qué come usted?*	What are you eating?
¿*Qué hace María?*	What is Maria doing?
¿*Qué dijo su maestro?*	What did your teacher say?

Quién (who, whom) or *quiénes* (pl) refers to persons only.

Examples:

¿Quién está con Antonio? — Who is with Anthony?
¿Quién tiene la bandera? — Who has the flag?
¿Con quiénes vive usted? — With whom do you live?
¿De quién habla ella? — Of whom is she speaking?

The verb always immediately follows *de quién* or *de quiénes* (whose) used as an interrogative.

Examples:

¿De quién es este perro? — Whose dog is this?
¿De quién es el lápiz? — Whose pencil is it?

When *de quién (-es)* is **not** used with the verb *ser* (to be), it has the following Spanish sentence construction: object/interrogative word/verb/ subject.

Example:

¿Los libros/de quién/ tiene/usted? — Whose books do you have?

Use *cuánto (-a)* (how much) and *cuántos (-as)* (how many) as a pronoun or adjective.

Examples:

¿Cuánto cuesta un pan dulce? — How much does a sweet roll cost?
¿Cuánto dinero gana usted? — How much money do you earn?
¿Cuántos van a la fiesta? — How many are going to the party?
¿Cuántas personas hay en su clase? — How many people are there in your class?

See Section I to review how relative pronouns can be made interrogative by the addition of a diacritic accent.

REPASO

Hay veinte y cinco estudiantes en la clase. Hay dos maestras. Una maestra se llama señora Gómez, la otra se llama señora Jones. La señora Gómez habla español e inglés y la señora Jones habla inglés. Algunos niños hablan español pero no hablan inglés. Otros alumnos hablan inglés pero no hablan español. Y, hay unos estudiantes que hablan español e inglés como la maestra. Los alumnos que hablan español van a aprender a leer primero en español y cuando hablan muy bien el inglés van a aprender a leer en inglés. Los estudiantes que hablan inglés van a aprender a leer en inglés primero, y cuando ellos aprenden a hablar bien en español ellos van a aprender a leer en español. Los estudiantes que hablan inglés y español van a aprender a leer en el idioma que hablan mejor.

¡Qué suerte tienen estos niños! ¡Pueden aprender a hablar y leer en dos idiomas! Pueden tener muchos amigos diferentes también.

Preguntas:

1. ¿Cuántos estudiantes hay en la clase?

2. ¿Cuántas maestras hay en la clase?

3. ¿Cómo se llaman las maestras?

4. ¿Cuál de las maestras habla español e inglés y cuál habla inglés?

5. ¿Cuáles niños van a aprender a leer en español?

6. ¿Quiénes van a aprender a leer en inglés?

7. ¿Cuándo van a aprender a leer en otro idioma los niños?

8. ¿En qué idioma van a aprender a leer los niños que hablan español e inglés?

9. ¿Por qué tienen suerte estos niños?

10. ¿Cuál es otra cosa buena de estar en esta clase?

Un niño pequeño entra en la escuela. Es su primer día. Está con su madre. El no sabe qué hacer ni a dónde ir. Su madre no sabe nada de esta escuela nueva. Hay una maestra en la clase. Quieren preguntarle algunas cosas pero la madre no habla inglés y el niño sólo habla un poco. El tiene miedo. En vez de hablar mal, él no dice nada. Ellos están esperando cerca de la puerta. La maestra les ve y les saluda. "Come in!" dice ella, pero la madre y el niño no se mueven. El niño comienza a llorar. No quiere quedarse en esta escuela donde no puede comunicar con nadie. Quiere quedarse en casa con su madre.

Cuando la maestra ve que el niño está llorando ella se da cuenta de que él no entiende lo que ella dice. Ella comienza a hablar en español.

"Buenos días. ¡Bienvenidos! ¡Favor de entrar en nuestra clase!"

Ahora, el niño tiene una sonrisa grande en la cara. Está contento. ¡Su madre ve que él está contento y ella vuelve a casa!

1. *¿A dónde va el niño pequeño?*

2. *¿Por qué no habla su madre?*

3. *¿Por qué no habla el niñito?*

4. *¿Qué dice la maestra primero?*

5. *¿Por qué no entran en la clase el niño y su madre?*

6. *¿Por qué llora el niñito?*

7. *¿Qué dice la maestra cuando ve que el niño está llorando?*

8. *¿Cómo cambia la cara del niño?*

9. *¿Por qué está contento?*

10. *¿A dónde va su madre?*

Verb Construction with Prepositions

After a preposition, when an -**ing** verb form occurs in English, use the full infinitive of the Spanish verb. Some common prepositions followed by an infinitive in Spanish are:

después de	after
antes de	before
desde	since
sin	without
por	through, for, on account of
para	for, in order to
al	on, upon
en vez de	instead of

Examples:

Después de aprenderlo se fué.	After learning it, he left.
Es importante escuchar bien antes de repetirlo.	It is important to listen carefully before repeating it.
Desde estar en nuestra clase, Juan está muy contento.	Since being in our class, Juan is very happy.
Es difícil leerlo sin oírlo primero.	It is difficult to read it without hearing it first.
El niño corrió por tener tanto frío.	The boy ran on account of being so cold.
Tenemos que estudiar para aprender.	We must study in order to learn.
Al entrar en la clase todos le saludaron en español.	Upon entering the class everyone greeted him in Spanish.
En vez de aprender a leer en inglés, aprendemos a leer en español.	Instead of learning to read in English we are learning to read in Spanish.

Idioms

An idiom is a whole expression whose meaning is not derivable from the conjoined meaning of the constituent parts. It is a complex lexical item and must be learned individually, preferably in a meaningful context. To really know a language one must know and be able to use and recognize its idioms.

Modismos útiles (Useful Idioms)

1. *darse cuenta de* - to realize, be aware of

   La maestra se da cuenta del problema.
   The teacher is aware of (realizes) the problem.

2. *de memoria* - by heart

   Los niños aprendieron de memoria las palabras.
   The children learned the words by heart.

3. *valer la pena* - to be worth(while), advantageous

   Vale la pena hablar dos idiomas.
   It's worthwhile to speak two languages.

4. *dar las gracias* - to thank, express gratitude, be grateful

   Antes de salir, le dí las gracias a mi amigo.
   Before leaving I thanked my friend.

5. *pensar en* - to think of, about, or over

   ¿En qué piensas?
   What are you thinking about?

6. *querer decir* - to mean

   ¿Qué quiere decir esa palabra?
   What does that word mean?

7. *poco a poco* - little by little, gradually, slowly, progressively

   Estoy aprendiendo el inglés poco a poco.
   Little by little I am learning English.

8. *tal vez* - perhaps, maybe, possibly, probably

   Tal vez mañana, Juanito.
   Perhaps tomorrow, Juanito.

9. *otra vez; de nuevo* - again, once more, another time

   Tiene que empezarlo de nuevo.
   You must start it again.

   Voy a hacerlo otra vez.
   I am going to do it again.

10. *Está bien o está bueno* - all right, OK, correct

    Cuando Juanito dijo: dos y dos son cuatro, su maestro respondió,
    --Está bien.

    When Juanito said, "2 and 2 are 4," his teacher responded,
    "Correct."

REPASO

I. *¿Cómo se dice en español?*

1. How many blocks are there in that box? _____

_____

2. I have just counted them and I know that there are twenty. _____

_____

3. What are you thinking about and what are you doing? _____

_____

4. Who has my book? Whose book do you have? _____

_____

5. Instead of visiting Luis at home, we can talk to him at the school.

_____

6. How many colors does the Mexican flag have and what colors are they?

_____

7. The children run through the streets without waiting for the traffic

light. _____

_____

8. The teacher has just explained the concept of sets to the class.

_____

9. We have just learned the alphabet in English. _____

_____

10. I didn't realize that you said "Thanks" before leaving. _____

_____

11. It's worthwhile learning the sounds and then you can gradually

understand the words. _____

_____

12. What does this sentence mean, Mrs. Jones? _____

_____

13. I don't want to do it to you again. _____

_____

14. The little girl closes her eyes and thinks (believes) that she is

hiding. _____

_____

15. There are many important people in our community. _____

_____

16. Whose pencil is this? _____

_____

17. It's Ana's pencil and she has just left. _____

_____

18. How many people are there in your family? _____

_____

19. What time is it and what's today's date? _____

_____

20. Who was the Aztec emperor when Cortés arrived in 1519? _____

_____

II. *Canciones*

Acabo de ver al cartero
(Tune: This Is The Way We Wash Our Clothes)

Acabo de ver al cartero, al cartero, al cartero
Acabo de ver al cartero
¿Qué hace él?
Lleva las cartas a mi casita, a mi casita, a mi casita
Lleva las cartas a mi casita
¡Qué suerte tengo yo!

Acabo de ver al médico, al médico, al médico
Acabo de ver al médico
¿Qué hace él?
Me ayuda a estar en buena salud, en buena salud, en buena salud
Me ayuda a estar en buena salud
¡Qué suerte tengo yo!

Acabo de ver al (bombero, policía, enfermero, lechero, basurero)
(¡Use su propia frase y repítala!)

La Finca de Paquito
(Tune: The House That Jack Built)

Mira la finca de Paquito

Mira la cebada
que se guarda en la finca de Paquito

Mira la rata
que comió la cebada
que se guarda en la finca de Paquito.

Mira la gata
que mató a la rata
que comió la cebada
que se guarda en la finca de Paquito.

Me Apunto a Mí Aquí

Me apunto a mí aquí, aquí   *(apuntar al pelo)*
Es el pelo, sí, mamá, sí
Pelo, sí, mamá, sí,
En la escuela lo aprendí   *(aplaudir dos veces)*

Me apunto a mí aquí, aquí   *(apuntar a los ojos)*
Son los ojos, sí, mamá, sí,
Ojos, sí, mamá, sí
En la escuela lo aprendí   *(aplaudir dos veces)*

Me apunto a mí aquí, aquí   *(apuntar a la nariz)*
Es la nariz, sí, mamá, sí
Nariz, sí, mamá, sí
En la escuela lo aprendí   *(aplaudir dos veces)*

Me apunto a mí aquí, aquí   *(apuntar a las orejas)*
Son las orejas, sí, mamá, sí
Orejas, sí, mamá, sí
En la escuela lo aprendí   *(aplaudir dos veces)*

Me apunto a mí aquí, aquí   *(apuntar a la boca)*
Es la boca, sí, mamá, sí
Boca, sí, mamá, sí
En la escuela lo aprendí   *(aplaudir dos veces)*

III. <u>Adivininanzas</u>

Acabo de comer algo
Era roja y dulce
¿Qué comí?
   (Una manzana)

Acabo de tomar algo
Era blanco
¿Qué tomé?
   (Leche)

IV. *¿Cómo se llama?*

¿Cómo se llama el hijo de su tía? _____

¿Cómo se llama la madre de su padre? _____

¿Cómo se llama el padre de su madre? _____

¿Cómo se llama la hermana de su padre? _____

¿Cómo se llama el hijo de su madre? _____

Forming the Imperfect Tense

To form the imperfect tense of first conjugation verbs *(-ar)*, add *-aba, -abas, -aba, -ábamos, -abais,* and *-aban* to the verb stem.

Examples:

cantar (stem: cant-)	
yo cantaba	I sang; I was singing, I used to sing
tú cantabas	You sang; you were singing; you used to sing
él, ella, Ud. cantaba	He, she, it, you sang; he, she, it, you were singing; he, she, it, you used to sing
nosotros cantábamos	We sang; we were singing; we used to sing
vosotros cantabais (fam pl)	You (fam pl) sang; you were singing; you used to sing
ellos, ellas, Uds. cantaban	They sang, they were singing; they used to sing

To form the imperfect tense of second *(-er)* and third *(-ir)* conjugation verbs, add *-ía, -ías, -ía, -íamos, -íais,* and *-ían* to the verb stem.

Modismos

comer (stem: com-)	
yo comía	I ate; I was eating, I used to eat
tú comías	You ate; you were eating; you used to eat
él, ella, Ud. comía	He, she, it, you ate; he, she, it, you were eating; he, she, it, you used to eat
nosotros comíamos	We ate; we were eating; we used to eat
vosotros comíais (fam pl)	You (fam pl) ate; you were eating; you used to eat
ellos, ellas, Uds. comían	They ate; they were eating; they used to eat

abrir (stem: abr-)

yo abría	I opened; I was opening; I used to open
tú abrías	You opened; you were opening; you used to open
él, ella, Ud. abría	He, she, it, you opened; he, she, it, you were opening; he, she, it, you used to open
nosotros abríamos	We opened; we were opening; we used to open
vosotros abríais (fam pl)	You (fam pl) opened; you were opening; you used to open
ellos, ellas, Uds. abrían	They opened; they were opening; they used to open

Using the Imperfect Tense

The imperfect indicative tense represents an action or condition taking place or existing in the past with no indication as to when the action or state began or ended. The activity of the state is actually imperfect; that is, unfinished or of indefinite duration. Its principle uses are:

√ To denote what was customary, habitual, or repeated in the past, usually translating the English used to, was accustomed to, or occasionally, would, followed by an infinitive.

Examples:

Ella vivía en Méjico.	She used to live in Mexico.
Su madre trabajaba en la escuela todos los miércoles.	Her mother worked at the school every Wednesday.
Quería hablar español todos los días.	She wanted to speak Spanish every day.

√ To describe actions and states in progress when something else was happening. Both verbs, in this case, are in the imperfect.

Examples:

Yo escuchaba mientras el maestro explicaba la lección.	I was listening while the teacher explained the lesson.
Los niños cantaban mientras la maestra tocaba el piano.	The children were singing while the teacher played the piano.

√ To describe an action which was in progress (imperfect) when another action took place (preterite).

Example:

> *El leía cuando la maestra*   He was reading when the teacher
> *entró.*   entered.

√ To express the time of day in the past.

Example:

> *Eran las seis.*   It was six o'clock.

√ To describe the background of an action, person, or thing in the past.

Examples:

> *Era un día despejado cuando*   It was a sunny day when the sun
> *salió el sol.*   rose.
> *Tenía el pelo negro.*   He had black hair.

Past Progressive

The use of the imperfect of *estar* plus a present participle expresses a continuous action in the past with no reference to its termination. It differs from the simple imperfect in that it emphasizes that the action was then actually in progress. (See Section X for a review of the present progressive and formation of participles.)

Example:

> *El estaba leyendo cuando*   He was reading when the teacher
> *la maestra entró.*   entered.

Irregular Imperfect Tense Verbs

The following verbs are irregular only in the imperfect tense and must be memorized:

ser: *era, eras, era, éramos, erais, eran*
ir: *iba, ibas, iba, íbamos, ibais, iban*
ver: *veía, veías, veía, veíamos, veíais, veían*

Examples:

1. *Fijarse en* - to notice, to pay attention to

   Un día el chivo se fijó en que había mucho zacate verde al otro lado del puente.
   One day the goat noticed that there was a lot of green grass on the other side of the bridge.

2. *ahora mismo* - at once, right away

   ¡Hágalo ahora mismo!
   Do it at once!

3. *Por lo menos, a lo menos* - at least

   Es necesario estudiar por lo menos una lección.
   It is necessary to study at least one lesson.

4. *Por fin, al fin* - at last, finally

   Por fin lo comprendió.
   At last he understood it.

5. *Tomar el pelo* - to deceive, pull one's leg (colloq.)

   Creo que me estás tomando el pelo.
   I think you're fooling me.

6. *Unos cuantos* - some, a few

   Déme unos cuantos dulces, por favor.
   Please give me some candies.

7. *Prestar atención* - to pay attention, be alert

   Es importante prestar atención en la clase.
   It is important to pay attention in class.

8. *Por la mitad* - in half, in the middle

   Parta usted esto por la mitad.
   Divide this in half.

9. *Ponerse de pie* - get up, stand, arise

   Cuando nuestra maestra entró, se pusieron todos de pie.
   When the teacher entered, everyone stood up.

10. *Ir de compras* - go shopping, do marketing

    María va de compras con su madre los jueves.
    María goes shopping with her mother on Thursdays.

REPASO

I. ¿Cómo se dice en español?

1. The cow was mooing and the donkey was braying when the farmer entered the barn. _____

   _____

2. It was 5:30 and the sun was rising. _____

   _____

3. We were singing and the teacher was playing the piano. _____

   _____

4. Last night I went to a party. _____

   _____

5. I used to visit my grandpa every Wednesday. _____

   _____

6. Paul was counting the blocks and I was reading a story when the bell rang. _____

   _____

7. We were listening carefully while the teacher explained the story.

   _____

8. She had black hair and black eyes and was very pretty. _____

   _____

9. I used to go to school with Pepe every day, or at least three times a week. _____

   _____

10. We were dividing the even numbers in half. _____

   _____

11. It was cold out and I was cold. _____

_____

12. They were paying attention to the teacher while she explained that there were many kinds of seeds. _____

_____

13. The teacher was telling us that air and rocks are minerals. _____

_____

14. Were you fooling me? _____

15. I saw Jaime every day and we used to eat lunch together. _____

_____

II. *Cuento*

Los Tres Chivos

Hace muchos años, había tres chivos que vivían en las montañas. Los tres chivos eran hermanos. Había el chivo grande, (poner al chivo grande al lado del puente) el chivo mediano, (poner al chivo mediano) y el chivo chiquito (poner al chivo chiquito).

A los chivos les gustaba mucho comer zacate. Un día se fijaron que del otro lado del puente había mucho zacate verde. Como el chivo chiquito tenía mucha hambre, pensó en ir para el otro lado del puente a comer de aquel zacate verde.

Comenzó a caminar, (hacer que el chivo chiquito cruce el puente) y cuando iba cruzando el puente se oían las pisadas en el puente (trip, trip, trip, trip, trip).

(susurrar) Pero los chivos no sabían que debajo del puente vivía un enano muy feo. Al oír las pisadas del chivo chiquito el enano brincó hacia el puente (hacer que el enano dé un brinco hacia el puente) y gritó con una voz ronca, "¿Quién va cruzando mi puente?"

"Soy yo, el chivo chiquito. Voy al otro lado a comer zacate para hacerme gordo."

"Voy a comerte," dijo el enano del puente.

"Por favor, señor, no me coma a mí. Yo soy muy chiquito. Espérese mejor hasta que pase mi hermano por aquí. El está mucho más gordo que yo."

"Bueno pues," dijo el enano, "pasa."

Poco más tarde el chivo mediano pensó ir al otro lado del puente donde veía a su hermanito comiendo zacate verde. Comenzó a cominar, pero cuando iba cruzando el puente se oían las pisadas en el puente. (trip-trap, trip-trap, trip-trap, trip-trap) Al oír las pisadas del chivo mediano, el enano dió un brinco hacia el puente y con voz ronca preguntó, "¿Quién va cruzando mi puente?"

"Soy yo, el chivo mediano. Voy al otro lado a comer zacate para hacerme más gordo. Voy a acompañar a mi hermanito."

"Voy a comerte," dijo el enano del puente.

"Por favor señor, no me coma a mí," dijo el chivo mediano. "Yo soy muy chico. Espérese mejor hasta que pase mi hermano grande por aquí. El está mucho más gordo que yo."

"Bueno pues," dijo el enano, "pasa."

Al fin el chivo grande decidió cruzar el puente a acompañar a sus hermanos. Pero cuando iba cruzando el puente se oían sus pisadas en el puente. (TRAP, TRAP, TRAP TRAP, TRAP TRAP, TRAP TRAP) El puente se mecía de tanto peso.

Al oír las pisadas y sentir que el puente se mecía, el enano brincó hacia el puente, y con voz ronca preguntó, "¿Quién va cruzando mi puente?"

"SOY YO," dijo el chivo grande. "VOY A ACOMPAÑAR A MIS HERMANOS QUE ESTÁN DEL OTRO LADO DE ESTE PUENTE."

"Voy a comerte," dijo el enano del puente.

"BUENO, VENTE," dijo el chivo grande. "YO TENGO DOS CUERNOS (poner los dedos sobre la cabeza) Y TE PUEDO SACAR LOS OJOS/TAMBIÉN TENGO ALGO DURO (tocar la frente) COMO UNA PIEDRA Y TE PUEDO HACER PEDACITOS."

El enano se acercó pero el chivo grande bajó la cabeza y con sus cuernos y su cabeza dura, le dió un golpe tan fuerte al enano que lo mandó por el aire y cayó en el agua. Allí se ahogó el enano y desde ese día en adelante, los chivos pudieron cruzar el puente cuando ellos quierían.

III. Canción

Allá en el Rancho Grande

Allá en el rancho grande,	--Te voy a hacer tus calzones,
allá donde vivía,	como los usa el ranchero,
había una rancherita,	te los comienzo de lana,
que alegre me decía,	te los acabo de cuero.
que alegre me decía:	

Allá en el rancho grande, etc.

--Te voy a hacer tu camisa,
como la usa el ranchero,
con el cuello a media espalda
y las mangas hasta el suelo.

Allá en el rancho grande, etc.

--Me enamoré de un ranchero
por ver si me daba elotes,
pero el ingrato ranchero
no me daba más que azotes.

Allá en el rancho grande, etc.

--Nunca te fíes de promesas
ni mucho menos de amores,
que si te dan calabazas
verás lo que son ardores.

Allá en el rancho grande, etc.

--Pon muy atento el oído
cuando rechine la puerta;
hay muertos que no hacen ruido
y son muy gordas sus penas.

Allá en el rancho grande, etc.

--Cuando te pidan cigarro
no des cigarro y cerillo,
porque si das las dos cosas
te tanterán de zorrillo.

Las Mañanitas

Estas son las mañanitas
que cantaba el rey David
Y hoy por ser día de tu santo
te las cantamos a ti.

Despierta, mi bien, despierta
mira que ya amaneció;
ya los pajarillos cantan
la luna ya se metió.

El día en que tú naciste
nacieron todas las flores;
y en la pila del bautismo
cantaron los ruiseñores.

Qué linda está la mañana
en que vengo a saludarte
venimos todos con gusto
y placer a felicitarte.

Feliz cumpleaños

Feliz cumpleaños a usted
Feliz cumpleaños a usted
Feliz cumpleaños a (nombre)
Feliz cumpleaños a usted.

IV. *Poema*

Ayer Me Fuí Al Campo

Ayer me fuí al campo,
¡Cómo me divertí!
Encontré a unas niñitas
que jugaban así.

El Granizo

El granizo de ayer tarde
muchas plantas destruyó.
¡Qué travieso es el granizo!
Tan travieso como yo.

En los vidrios azotaba
y algunos los rompió.
¡Qué travieso es el granizo!
Tan travieso como yo.

En la tarde hicimos nieve
del granizo que cayó,
con azúcar y limones
muy sabrosa que quedó.

V. *Poesía*

Había una ancianita

Había una ancianita
y en una chancla vivía.

Tenía tantas criaturas
que ya loca se volvía.

Los alimentaba con frijolitos
mantequilla y panecitos.

Para dormir los arrullaba,
y en sus camitas los acostaba.

VI. *Otro cuento*

El Chivito Que Quería Ser Niño

Una vez, había un chivito que quería ser niño. El iba a la escuela
todos los días y veía a los niños jugar. El quería ser como ellos e ir a
la escuela a jugar con ellos, pero se quedaba afuera de la cerca y veía a
los niños jugar, tristemente. . .

--¡Yo sé qué hacer!-- dijo el chivito un día. --Me voy a poner ropa
y voy a hacerme niño. El chivito corrió a su casa y se puso unos pantalones
azules, una camisa verde, unos calcetines amarillos y unos zapatos cafés.
Salió al prado muy feliz porque el creía que ya era un niño. En un árbol
estaba Don Buho Sabio. El Buho le dijo al chivito:

--Oye, chivito, ¿Por qué te has puesto esos pantalones, esa camisa
y esos zapatos y esos calcetines?

--Porque ahora soy niño-- dijo el chivito.

--Ja, ja, ja,-- reía el buho, diciéndole, --Tú no eres niño, chivito.

El chivito, muy desanimado, se fue muy triste hacia su casa porque
todavía no era niño. Pero de pronto se sonrió.

--¡Ya sé qué hacer!-- dijo el chivito. --Si no puedo ser niño, entonces
voy a ser niña. Corrió a su casa y de una caja que tenía su mamá sacó una
falda, una blusa, unas medias y unos zapatos negros. Se quitó la ropa que
traía y se puso esta otra. Luego se fue muy alegre a la pradera. El chivito
creía que él era niña. Allí en el prado estaba su papá, el chivo grande.

--Hijito,-- le dijo su papá, --¿Qué haces con esa falda y esa blusa y
esos calcetines, y esos zapatos de niña?

--Yo quiero ser niña, papá,-- dijo el chivito. --Yo soy una niña
ahora porque me he vestido como niña.

--¿Por qué quieres ser niña?

--Porque yo quiero jugar con los niños y las niñas que están allá en
la escuela-- respondió el chivito.

--Mira, hijito,-- dijo el chivo grande. --Porque traes prendas de
vestir no te haces niño. Tú eres un chivito muy bonito. ¿Por qué no te
quitas la ropa de niña, te limpias tu piel y vas a jugar con los niños?
Si eres niño, vas a ser feo porque tú no naciste como niño, pero si tú eres
chivito, eres un chivito muy bonito.

El chivito se quitó la ropa y se fue a jugar con los niños.

Todos dijeron--Miren que chivito tan bonito. Vamos a jugar con él.

A partir de entonces el chivito fue muy feliz siendo un chivito como
era y no un niño. Por fin estaba contento con ser lo que su mamá y su papá
le hicieron.

Using *Gustar*

Use *gustar* (to please or to give pleasure) when expressing <u>to like</u> for which there is no exact equivalent in Spanish. To use *gustar* for <u>to like</u>, reverse the English construction so that the English object becomes the Spanish subject and the English subject becomes the Spanish indirect object. The word order for verbs like *gustar* is: indirect object/verb/subject. The simplest way to understand this is to think of <u>to like</u> as meaning <u>to be pleasing</u> or <u>to appeal to</u>.

Examples:

Me gustan esas flores.	<u>I like those flowers</u>. (Those flowers are pleasing to me. Those flowers appeal to me.)
Le gusta Arizona.	<u>He likes Arizona</u>. (Arizona is pleasing to him. Arizona appeals to him.)

Use the third person singular or plural to agree with the subject and note that the subject usually follows the verb *gustar*. In negative sentences, *no* always precedes the indirect object pronoun.

Examples:

Le gusta la clase.	<u>He likes the class</u>. (The class is pleasing to him.)
No le gusta la clase.	<u>He doesn't like the class</u>. (The class doesn't appeal to him.)

Since the English object becomes the Spanish subject, it is generally necessary to insert an article before the Spanish subject.

Examples:

Me gustan las legumbres.	<u>I like vegetables</u>. (Vegetables are pleasing to me.)
A los niños les gusta la leche.	<u>Children like milk</u>. (Milk is pleasing to the children.)

Since the English subject becomes the Spanish indirect object, it must be accompanied by its corresponding indirect object pronoun (*me, te, le, nos, os,* or *les*), and must be introduced by the preposition *a* if it is a noun.

Example:

A María le gusta el libro.   <u>Maria likes the book</u>. (The book
                                is pleasing to Maria.)

Use *a* and a prepositional pronoun to clarify the meaning of *le* or
les when the meaning is not clear from the context.

Example:

(A él) le gusta la música.   <u>He likes the music</u>. (The music
                                is pleasing to him.)

Use *gustar* to express <u>to like</u>, indicating fondness for a certain
action. Use the infinitive as the sentence's subject and the third person
singular of *gustar*.

Example:

Nos gusta estudiar.   <u>We like to study</u>. (To study is
                                pleasing to us.)

Gustar is not generally applied to liking people. The closest idiom
to express the idea of liking someone is *caer bien*. To express dislike,
use *caer mal*. The same reversal of object and subject occurs with these
idioms as with *gustar*.

Examples:

Me cae bien ese maestro.   <u>I like that teacher</u>. (That
                                teacher is pleasing to me.)

Me cae mal ese maestro.   <u>I don't like that teacher</u>. (That
                                teacher is not pleasing to me.)

NOTE: *Gustar* may be used in the past tense also.

Using *Faltar*

The verb *faltar* (to lack or to need) corresponds to *gustar* in all
respects. It is not as important as the verb *gustar* since, for all practical
purposes, *faltar* can be replaced by *necesitar*. At least a passing knowledge
of *faltar* should be helpful in understanding it when it is used by others.

Example:

Le faltan cinco dólares para   <u>He needs (lacks) five dollars</u>
   comprar el boleto.   <u>to buy the ticket</u>. (Five
                                dollars to buy the ticket
                                are lacking to him.)

Other verbs that follow the pattern of *gustar* and *faltar* are:

interesar	to interest
parecer	to seem
quedar	to have (something) left

Modismos

1. <u>*Tener en cuenta*</u> - to keep in mind, consider

   Tenga en cuenta los sonidos que la maestra señaló.
   Keep in mind the sounds that the teacher pointed out.

2. <u>*Contar con*</u> - to depend upon, count on

   Cuento con su ayuda.
   I'm counting on your help.

3. <u>*Pensar de*</u> - to think of, have an opinion of or about

   ¿Qué piensas de Pepe?
   What do you think of Pepe?

4. <u>*Por supuesto*</u> - of course, certainly

   ¿Habla usted español?   ¡Por supuesto!
   Do you speak Spanish? Of course!

5. <u>*Preocuparse por*</u> - to worry about, be concerned for or about

   No te preocupes por Juan.
   Don't worry about Juan.

6. <u>*Alegrarse de*</u> - to be glad or happy about (something)

   Me alegro mucho de verla.
   I am very happy to see her.

7. <u>*Hacerse tarde*</u> - to become late, be getting (or growing) late

   Cuando se pone el sol, sabemos que se hace tarde.
   When the sun sets, we know it's getting late.

8. <u>*Poner la mesa*</u> - to set the table

   Ayudo a mi madre cuando pone la mesa.
   I help my mother when she sets the table.

9. <u>*Sobre todo*</u> - especially, particularly, above all

   Me gusta el postre sobre todo si hay helados.
   I like dessert, especially if there is ice cream.

10. _Parecido a_ - like, similar to

Tengo un color muy parecido a ese color.
I have a color very similar to that color.

REPASO

I. _¿Cómo se dice en español?_

1. We like the games that we play in school. _____

_____

2. Do you like your class? _____

3. They have three colors left. How many colors do you have left,

Angel? _____

_____

4. The sounds of the vowels interest me. _____

_____

5. It seems to me that you like to sing. _____

_____

6. We like to play with the animals, but we don't like to bother them

when it's hot. _____

_____

7. Did you like your trip? _____

8. Which do you like more, ice cream or carrots? _____

_____

9. The teacher likes to wear a hat. _____

_____

10. I need fifty cents because I want to buy many things. _____

_____

II. *¡Ponga usted la forma correcta de gustar!*

1. _____ *el helado* (he likes)

2. _____ *el libro* (you [pl.] like)

3. _____ *la casa* (we like)

4. _____ *el chocolate* (I like)

5. _____ *las manzanas* (she likes)

III. <u>*Un cuento*</u>

El Pollito

Esta es la historia de un pollito, un pollito bonito y gracioso. Un día este pollito tenía mucha hambre. Fué al jardín para buscar algo que comer. Buscaba algo bueno por todas partes. Encontró un gusano. Al pollito le gustan mucho los gusanos.

Al pollito sí le gustan los gusanos. El pollito estaba muy ocupado comiendo el gusano cuando una hoja, una hoja muy grande, una hoja inmensa, le cae en la cabeza. El pobre pollito tenía miedo. Creía que el cielo se estaba cayendo. Y corrió gritando:

--¡Pío, pío, pío, pío! ¡Mamacita! ¡Mamacita! ¿Dónde estás, mamacita?

--Clo, clo, clo, clo, aquí estoy, hijo mío,-- dice la gallina, la madre del pollito, --¿Qué pasa?

--¡El cielo se está cayendo!

--¿Cómo lo sabes, hijo?

--Lo ví con mis propios ojos y un pedazo me cayó ¡pum! ¡sobre la cabeza!

--¡Corramos!-- gritó la gallina. --¡Corramos! ¡Corramos!

--¡Pato! ¡Pato! ¿Dónde estás, Pato?

--¡Cuac, cuac, cuac, cuac! Aquí estoy gallina. ¿Qué pasa? ¿Qué pasa?

--¡El cielo se está cayendo!

--¿Cómo lo sabes, gallina?

--*Me lo dijo el pollito.*

--*¿Cómo lo sabes, pollito?*

--*Lo ví con mis propios ojos y un pedazo me cayó ¡pum! sobre la cabeza.*

--*¡Corramos!-- grita el pato. ¡Corramos! ¡Corramos!*

--*¡Ganso! ¡Ganso! ¿Dónde estás, ganso?*

--*¡Juanc, juanc, juanc, juanc! Aquí estoy, pato. ¿Qué pasa? ¿Qué pasa?*

--*¡El cielo se está cayendo!*

--*¿Cómo lo sabes, Pato?*

--*Me lo dijo la gallina.*

--*¿Cómo lo sabes, gallina?*

--*Me lo dijo el pollito.*

--*¿Cómo lo sabes, pollito?*

--*Lo ví con mis propios ojos y un pedazo me cayó, ¡pum! sobre la cabeza.*

--*¡Corramos!-- grita el ganso. --¡Corramos! ¡Corramos!*

--*¡Guajolote! ¡Guajolote! ¿Dónde estás, guajolote?*

--*¡Gaubul, gaubul, gaubul, gaubul! Aquí estoy, ganso. ¿Qué pasa? ¿Qué pasa?*

--*¡El cielo se está cayendo!*

--*¿Cómo lo sabes, pato?*

--*Me lo dijo la gallina.*

--*¿Cómo lo sabes, gallina?*

--*Me lo dijo el pollito.*

--*¿Cómo lo sabes, pollito?*

--*¡Lo ví con mis propios ojos y un pedazo me cayó ¡pum! sobre la cabeza.*

--¡Corramos!-- grita el guajolote. ¡Corramos! ¡Corramos!

--¡Zorra! ¡Zorra! ¿Dónde estás, zorra?

--¡Grr, grr, grr, grr! Aquí estoy, guajolote. ¿Qué pasa? ¿Qué pasa?

--¡El cielo se está cayendo!

--¿Cómo lo sabes, ganso?

--Me lo dijo el pato.

--¿Cómo lo sabes, pato?

-- Me lo dijo la gallina.

--¿Cómo lo sabes, gallina?

--Me lo dijo el pollito.

--¿Cómo lo sabes, pollito?

--Lo ví con mis propios ojos y un pedazo me cayó ¡pum! sobre la cabeza.

La zorra piensa un momentito y entonces dice:

--No tengan ustedes miedo. Yo les salvaré. Vengan a mi cueva. Vengan conmigo.

El pollito, la gallina, el pato, el ganso y el guajolote siguen a la zorra. Los animales llegan a la cueva. La zorra dice:

--Pasen ustedes. Pasen ustedes. Esta es su casa.

El pollito, la gallina, el pato, el ganso y el guajolote dicen:

--¡Muchas gracias! ¡Con permiso! y entran en la cueva de la zorra. ¡Y fíjense ustedes! La zorra, este animal cruel, se come al pollito; la zorra se come a la gallina; la zorra se come al pato; la zorra se come al ganso y la zorra se come al guajolote. ¡Pobres animales!

Y después de comer a todos los animales esta zorra tan cruel y tan mala sale de su cueva y dice:

--Mmmm ¡Qué buena comida!

SECTION XV

The prepositions *por* and *para* have such a close resemblance and are so frequently translated alike in English that it is necessary to study their uses carefully to know which one to use in Spanish. Each preposition has definite uses and cannot be interchanged for the other without altering the meaning of a sentence.

Using *Para*

Use *para* to express <u>for</u>, meaning destined for, for the purpose of, in order to, used for, for a time in the future, and considering the fact that.

Examples:

El sale para Mexico.	He is leaving for Mexico.
Comemos para vivir.	We eat to (in order to) live.
Es una caja para creyones.	It is a box for crayons.
El tiene una cita para el lunes.	He has an appointment for Monday.
Para un niñito comprende muy bien las matemáticas.	For a little boy, he understands math very well.

Using *Por*

Use *por* to express <u>for</u>, meaning in exchange for, for the sake of, and for a period of.

Examples:

Pagó cinco dólares por el libro.	He paid five dollars for the book.
El peleaba por la vida.	He was fighting for his life.
No habló por dos minutos.	He didn't speak for two minutes.

Use *por* to express <u>by</u> or <u>through</u> and <u>by means of</u>.

Examples:

El entró por la puerta.	He entered through the door.
Viajaron a la escuela por camión.	They travelled to school by bus.

Use *por* to mean <u>for</u> following the verbs *ir*, *enviar*, and *luchar*.

Examples:

Voy por el libro.	<u>I am going for the book.</u>
Envió por la información.	<u>He sent for the information.</u>
El pajarito estaba luchando *por la vida.*	<u>The little bird was fighting for</u> <u>his life.</u>

Do not translate <u>for</u> with these verbs: *esperar* (to wait for), *buscar* (to look for), and *pedir* (to ask for). The word <u>for</u> is incorporated in the meaning of the verb.

Example:

Busco el libro.	<u>I'm looking for the book.</u>

Use the prepositional pronouns after *por* or *para*. Subject or personal pronouns (listed in Section II) also function as prepositional pronouns except that *yo* becomes *mí* and *tú* becomes *ti*. The other forms remain the same.

Special expressions with *por*:

por cierto	by the way
por ejemplo	for example
por eso	that's why
por supuesto	of course
por favor	please
por fin	finally, at last
por lo menos	at least
por poco	almost

Using *Hace Que* to Indicate Time

Hace plus a <u>time expression</u> plus *que* followed by a verb in the present tense indicates the length of time an action <u>has been</u> (and still is) going on.

Examples:

Hace tres meses que asisto
   a esta escuela.
	<u>I have been attending this school</u>
	   <u>for three months.</u> (It makes
	   three months that I have been
	   attending this school.)

¿Cuánto tiempo hace que
   está en Arizona?
	<u>How long have you been in Arizona?</u>
	   (How much time does it make that
	   you are in Arizona?)

Hacía plus a time expression plus *que* followed by a verb in the imperfect tense indicates the length of time an action had been (and was still) taking place.

Examples:

Hacía dos años que le conocíamos al maestro.	We had known the teacher for two years. (It made two years that we knew the teacher.)
¿Cuánto tiempo hacía que usted conocía a Luis?	How long had you known Luis? (How much time did it make that you knew Luis?)

Hace plus a period of time following a verb in the preterite or imperfect tense means ago.

Examples:

La carta llegó hace tres horas.	The letter arrived three hours ago.
Le ví hace dos días.	I saw him two days ago.

Modismos

1. asistir a - to attend

   Yo asisto a esa escuela.
   I attend that school.

2. conocer (a una persona) - to know (a person)

   ¿Conoces a Roberto? Sí, le conozco.
   Do you know Roberto? Yes, I know him.

3. por primera vez - for the first time

   Por primera vez puedo hablar español sin pensar en cada palabra.
   For the first time I can speak Spanish without thinking about every word.

4. dar una vuelta, dar un paseo - take a walk, take a stroll

   Quiero dar una vuelta antes de volver a casa.
   I want to take a walk before returning home.

5. echar de menos a una persona - to miss a person

   ¡Te echo de menos!
   I miss you!

REPASO

I. *¿Cómo se dice en español?*

1. How long have you lived in Arizona? _____

    _____

2. I have studied Spanish for two years. _____

    _____

3. The seeds travel through the air by water and wind. _____

    _____

4. How long have you been travelling by plane? _____

    _____

5. We are leaving for Mexico tomorrow. _____

    _____

6. We haven't been there for a long time. _____

    _____

7. I am studying in order to learn. _____

    _____

8. I finished the lesson ten minutes ago. _____

    _____

9. The bird flew through the window and almost broke it. _____

    _____

10. How long had you been attending that school when you left Mexico?

    _____

    _____

11. He paid ten dollars for the books. _____

    _____

12. We are waiting for the bus to go to school. _____

_____

13. I have been looking for that book for two hours. _____

_____

14. The teacher gave me ten crayons to draw the animals. _____

_____

15. We use our eyes to see. _____

II. Conteste usted en español

1. ¿Cuántos meses hace que usted estudia español? _____

_____

2. ¿Cuánto tiempo hacía que conocía a Juan antes de llegar aquí?

_____

3. ¿Qué tiempo hace hoy? _____

4. ¿Cómo se llama su escuela y cuánto tiempo hace que la asiste?

_____

5. ¿Para qué usamos las pinturas? _____

_____

III. Escoja usted por o para.

1. _____ un recién llegado, usted habla inglés muy bien.

2. Vamos a la escuela _____ camión.

3. ¿_____ qué usamos la nariz?

4. Mi madre pagó diez dólares _____ los alimentos.

5. Tengo diez centavos _____ comprar unos dulces.

IV. ¿Puede usted escribir un diálogo entre una maestra y un alumno de su
clase? Ella quiere explicarle la importancia del maíz.

V. *Poema*

Los Sentidos

Niño, vamos a cantar una bonita canción
yo te voy a preguntar; tú me vas a responder.
Los ojos, ¿para qué son? Los ojos son para ver.
Y ¿el tacto? Para tocar. Y ¿el oído? Para oír.
Y ¿el olfato? Para oler. Y ¿el gusto? Para gustar.
¿El alma? Para sentir, para querer y pensar.

Quiero Ser

Quiero ser una flor
para darla a mi amor;
Quiero ser caracol
para dormir en el sol.

Quiero ser la media luna
y cantarle una runa.
Quiero ser un mal pirata
en buen barco de lata.

VI. *Canción*

La Bamba

¡Para bailar la bamba, para bailar la bamba, para bailar la bamba
se necesita una poca de gracia y otra cosita!
Bamba, bamba, bamba, bamba, bamba, bamba, bamba, bamba
¡Para bailar la bamba, para bailar la bamba,
para bailar la bamba se necesita una poca de gracia y otra cosita!
¡Ay arriba y arriba y arribe iré! Yo no soy marinero, por tí seré.
Bamba, bamba, bamba, bamba, bamba, bamba, bamba, bamba

Una vez que te dije, una vez que te dije, una vez que te dije
que fuiste hermosa, se te puso la cara color de rosa.
¡Ay arriba y arriba! ¡Y arriba iré! Yo no soy marinero, por
tí seré.
Bamba, bamba . . . .

¡Ay, te pido, te pido! ¡Ay te pido, te pido! ¡Ay, te pido,
te pido de compasión que se acabe la bamba y venga otro son!
¡Ay arriba y arriba y arriba iré!
Yo no soy marinero, por tí seré.

Bamba, bamba, bamba, bamba,
Bamba, bamba, bamba . . . .

VII. *Días de fiesta*

El Día de Todos los Santos

Le gente de habla española siempre tiene su modo especial de celebrar
las fiestas y de divertirse. Así es que la fiesta del Día de Todos los
Santos no es nada parecida a la fiesta norteamericana del treinta y uno de
octubre. Para ellos es una fiesta religiosa. En países hispanos hay dos
días de fiesta. El primero de noviembre es el Día de Todos los Santos, y
el dos de noviembre es el Día de los Difuntos (dead). Aunque son fiestas
religiosas son muy alegres.

En México hay dos días de fiesta para los muertos. En la fiesta
mexicana existen elementos pintorescos que son netamente mexicanos.

¡El treinta y uno de octubre en la bella Ciudad de México! Comenzando
en esta noche por quince días se presenta DON JUAN TENORIO en los teatros.
De los campos vienen los indios y ponen en las calles y en las alamedas
puestos en que venden calaveras (skulls) chiquitas de barro. No se encuen-
tran sino durante esta celebración. También hay puestos que venden máscaras
(masks) y otros que venden tarjetas postales con versos graciosos acerca de
los muertos. También se venden pasteles y dulces en forma de calaveras,
esqueletos (skeletons) y otras cosas.

En lòs dos días va la gente a los cementerios (cemeteries) a visitar
las tumbas de los muertos. Llevan flores y velas. Todos rezan por el alma
de los difuntos. Después algunos van a divertirse de algún modo. Otros van
a misa y más tarde a las corridas de toros, al cabaret a bailar, al teatro
a ver DON JUAN TENORIO o a la casa de algun amigo.

Navidad en los Países de Habla Española

En España, la gente goza en bailar durante el tiempo de Navidad.
Después de misa de media noche en la Nochebuena, las calles pronto se llenan
con bailadores y espectadores. Las palabras y la música del baile de Navidad,
conocido como la "Jota," han sido transmitidas por cientos de años. Los
españoles le llaman a la réplica en miniatura de Belén "el Nacimiento."

En México, la temporada de Navidad dura desde el día 16 de diciembre
hasta el día 6 de enero. Cada familia anticipa con placer "la posada" en
cada una de las nueve noches antes del día de Navidad. Los miembros de la
familia hacen el papel de la posada en memoria de la búsqueda de posada por
María y José en la primera Nochebuena. Forman una procesión de cuarto a
cuarto, guiada por dos niños que cargan las figuras de María y José. En la
puerta de cada cuarto, los niños piden posada, pero se les niega. Cuando
llegan al cuarto del altar, los niños son admitidos. Ponen las figuras de
María y José en el establo de la réplica en miniatura de Belén. No ponen
la figura del infante Jesús en el pesebre hasta la Nochebuena, la última
noche de la posada. Una hora social sigue a la última posada. El huésped
invita a todos al patio para que ayuden a quebrar la piñata que está hecha
de un jarro o de papel majado, decorado alegremente y lleno de regalos y
dulces. Cuelga de un cordón del techo o de la rama de un árbol. Se les
vendan los ojos a los niños y ellos toman turnos tratando de quebrar la
piñata con un palo. Cuando se quiebra, los regalos y dulces caen y los
niños corren a recogerlos.

En Guatemala y Honduras, los niños también disfrutan de la piñata. La
gente usa flores en lugar de siempreverdes para decoraciones en muchos de los
países donde la Navidad viene durante la temporada cálida. La flor de Noche
Buena florece en México durante la Navidad.

En Sur América, muchos de los niños creen que los reyes magos les
traen los regalos de Navidad.

Los niños de Brasil y Argentina hallan regalos en sus zapatos en la
mañana de Navidad. En la víspera de Epifanía, día duodécimo después de Navidad,
ellos dejan agua y paja en el escalón de la puerta para los camellos de los
reyes magos.

La gente de Chile tiene una fiesta en el día de Navidad. Es como una
feria en los Estados Unidos.

Los Indios de los países de Sur América tienen una fiesta durante la
temporada de la Navidad.

En Puerto Rico, muchas familias celebran la Nochebuena con cenas, música y baile. Los niños reciben regalos en Navidad y otra vez en la mañana de la Epifanía, el 6 de enero. Los Nacimientos se ven en iglesias y edificios públicos.

The Future Indicative Tense

To form the future indicative tense of *-ar*, *-er*, and *-ir* regular verbs, add the following endings to the <u>entire infinitive</u>: *-é*, *-ás*, *-á*, *-emos*, *-éis* and *-án*.

Examples:

hablar	<u>to speak</u>
hablaré	<u>I shall speak</u>
hablarás	<u>you will speak</u>
hablará	<u>he, she, you will speak</u>
hablaremos	<u>we shall speak</u>
hablaréis	<u>you will speak</u>
hablarán	<u>they, you (pl) will speak</u>
aprender	<u>to learn</u>
aprenderé	<u>I shall learn</u>
aprenderás	<u>you will learn</u>
aprenderá	<u>he, she, you will learn</u>
aprenderemos	<u>we shall learn</u>
aprenderéis	<u>you will learn</u>
aprenderán	<u>they, you (pl) will learn</u>
ir	<u>to go</u>
iré	<u>I shall go</u>
irás	<u>you will go</u>
irá	<u>he, she, you will go</u>
iremos	<u>we will go</u>
iréis	<u>you will go</u>
irán	<u>they, you (pl) will go</u>

Irregular Future Indicative Tense Verbs

There are twelve irregular verbs in the future indicative tense.

√ In the first five verbs, drop the vowel of the infinitive endings.

caber: <u>to contain, to fit into</u>
    cabré, cabrás, cabrá, cabremos, cabréis, cabrán
haber: <u>to have</u>
    habré, habrás, habrá, habremos, habréis, habrán
poder: <u>to be able</u>
    podré, podrás, podrá, podremos, podréis, podrán
querer: <u>to want, wish</u>
    querré, querrás, querrá, querremos, querréis, querrán
saber: <u>to know</u>
    sabré, sabrás, sabrá, sabremos, sabréis, sabrán

√ In the next five verbs, change the vowel of the infinitive ending to
d before attaching the regular endings.

poner: to put, place
  pondré, pondrás, pondrá, pondremos, pondréis, pondrán
salir: to leave
  saldré, saldrás, saldrá, saldremos, saldréis, saldrán
tener: to have
  tendré, tendrás, tendrá, tendremos, tendréis, tendrán
valer: to be worth
  valdré, valdrás, valdrá, valdremos, valdréis, valdrán
venir: to come
  vendré, vendrás, vendrá, vendremos, vendréis, vendrán

√ In the last two verbs, delete *ec* and *ce* from the infinitive.

decir: to say, tell
  diré, dirás, dirá, diremos, diréis, dirán
hacer: to do, to make
  haré, harás, hará, haremos, haréis, harán

Probability or Conjecture

In addition to expressing future time, the future tense may be used
instead of the present indicative tense to express probability or conjecture.

Examples:

Juan no está aquí; estará en la otra clase.	Juan is not here; he is probably in the other class.
El niño no comió nada; tendrá hambre.	The boy ate nothing; he must be hungry.

Habrá

Use *habrá* to mean there will be or there shall be.

Example:

Creo que habrá muchos niños aquí mañana.	I think there will be many children here tomorrow.

Ir A

The present indicative tense of the verb *ir* plus *a* preceding an
infinitive may replace the Spanish future tense.

Examples:

Voy a comer a las doce.	I am going to eat at twelve.
Comeré a las doce.	I shall eat at twelve.
Voy a estudiar esta noche.	I am going to study tonight.
Estudiaré esta noche.	I shall study tonight.

From the preceding examples, it is apparent that the English and Spanish use of the future tense and the verb <u>to go</u> in the present indicative tense plus an infinitive express much the same idea. The future is included so that you will be familiar with it when it is used by others. For all practical purposes, it can be replaced by *ir* plus *a* plus <u>an infinitive</u>.

Examples:

Voy a hablarle en español.	I'm going to speak to you in Spanish.
Vamos a leer un cuento.	We are going to read a story.

Colloquially, *vamos a* plus <u>an infinitive</u> also means <u>let's</u>.

Examples:

Vamos a cantar.	Let's sing.
Vamos a ver.	Let's see.

Present Tense Used as Future Tense

It is common to translate the present tense as the future tense.

Examples:

Lo hago mañana.	I'll do it tomorrow.
¿Abro el libro?	Shall I open the book?

Relative Pronouns

While in English relative pronouns are often omitted, they are never omitted in Spanish. The most commonly used relative pronoun in Spanish is *que*, which may refer to persons or things. *Que* may be a subject or an object.

Examples:

La maestra que acaba de entrar habla español.	The teacher who has just entered speaks Spanish.
El libro que acabo de leer era muy interesante.	The book that I have just read was very interesting.

After a preposition *quien* replaces *que* when referring to person.

Example:

El hombre con quien hablé   The man with whom I spoke was nice.
   era simpático.

When the antecedent refers to a general idea, action, or situation rather than to a specific masculine or feminine word, the neuter form *lo que* (or *lo cual*) is used.

Examples:

El niño no comprendió   The boy didn't understand what his
   lo que dijo su maestro.   teacher said.
No sé lo que me falta.   I don't know what's missing.

Modismos

1. *Dentro de* - inside (of); in or within (a period of time)

   Dentro de unas semanas comprenderá todo.
   Within a few weeks you will understand everything.

2. *A fondo* - thoroughly, fully

   El niño explicó a fondo todo el concepto.
   The child thoroughly explained the entire concept.

3. *Delante de* - in the presence of, in front of

   ¡No te portes así delante de tu maestra!
   Don't behave that way in front of your teacher!

4. *Detrás de* - behind

   Los libros están detrás de la caja de bloques.
   The books are behind the carton of blocks.

5. *Dejar de* - stop, cease

   Deje de hablar de esas cosas.
   Stop talking about those things.

6. *De ninguna manera* - by no (any) means, under no (any) circumstances

   No podrá ir de ninguna manera.
   You will not be able to go under any circumstances.

7. _De enfrente_ - across (the street), directly opposite, in front (of)

   Viven en la casa de enfrente.
   They live in the house across the street.

8. _Sin querer_ - unwittingly, unintentionally

   Los niños lo dijeron sin querer.
   The children said it unintentionally.

9. _Faltar a_ - to absent one's self from, miss, "cut" a class

   Juan faltó a la clase ayer.
   Juan cut class yesterday.

10. _Al revés_ - the contrary, opposite; inside out

    La historia no es así, precisamente es al revés.
    The story doesn't go that way, it is exactly the opposite.

REPASO

I. _¿Cómo se dice en español?_

1. The teacher who is near the door will read the story. _____

   _____

2. Luis is not in class today. He's probably sick. _____

   _____

3. I will understand what you're saying within a few weeks. _____

   _____

4. Will those blocks fit into the set? _____

   _____

5. I will have to arrange them in a square. _____

   _____

6. You will not be able to do everything today, but we will finish it

   tomorrow. _____

   _____

7. You will sit in this seat and use these pencils and crayons.

_____

8. No one understands the lesson. It is probably too difficult.

_____

9. The teacher will play the piano and we will sing. _____

_____

10. Let's read a story now and let's rest later. _____

_____

11. If you listen carefully and watch my lips, it will be easier to

repeat the sound. _____

_____

12. Let's see! What will we do first? _____

_____

13. I like to paint and draw. Will you help me? _____

_____

14. When we practice math, it will be necessary to close your book.

_____

15. I don't know what I did, but he thoroughly understands the concept.

_____

16. He stopped talking in front of the teacher. _____

_____

17. Does David cut the class frequently? On the contrary, he is never

absent. _____

_____

18. I said it unwittingly and within a few minutes the little boy

started to cry. _____

_____

19. Will you wait for me across the street? _____

_____

20. Will we learn only English? On the contrary, we will learn Spanish and English. _____

_____

II. *Poesía*

     Huevo, Huevito

     Huevo, Huevito, muy sentadito
     en la alta cerca;
     Huevo, Huevito, te vas a caer.

     Todos los caballos
     y hombres del rey
     nunca, nunca te podrán componer.

III. *Canciones*

Los Tres Gatitos

     Los tres gatitos perdieron sus guantecitos
     y se pusieron a llorar.
     Mamá, mamá, tenemos que confesar
     que los guantes no podemos hallar.

¡Qué malos gatitos, perder los guantecitos!
Por eso, no tendréis pastel.
Miau, miau, miau, miau.
¡Pues no, no tendréis pastel!

Los tres gatitos encontraron sus guantecitos
y de nuevo se pusieron a llorar.
Mamá, mamá, ya te podemos avisar
que los acabamos de encontrar.

Pónganse los guantecitos, majaderos gatitos,
y os daré un pastel.
Ronron, ronron, ronron, ronron.
¡Qué rico es nuestro pastel!

IV. Cuento con moraleja

Las Dos Jaibas

Un día dos jaibas salieron de casa para pasearse en la arena.
--Hija,-- le dice la mamá a la jaiba pequeña, --caminas con tan poca
gracia.-- Debes acostumbrarte a andar derecha y no a menearte de lado
a lado. --Pero mamá,-- le contesta la jaiba, --póngame el ejemplo y yo
lo seguiré.

¿Qué moraleja tiene esta fábula? (El ejemplo es la mejor ley.)

V. Poema

El Maíz

Sembramos con alegría
los granitos de maíz.
En ricas tierras con cariño,
serán un porvenir.

Probaremos rico pozole
con tortillas que hace mamá,
tamalitos frescos, pinole,
que el maíz nos ofrecerá.

Y ya vemos los maizales
muy alegres.
Los cosecharemos ya muy pronto,
el maíz de nuestro afán.

VI. *Cuento*

Pregúntale Al Señor Oso

Había un niño que se llamaba Daniel. Daniel estaba sentado en los escalones de su casa, pensando, pensando - ¿qué le daré a mi mamá para su cumpleaños? ¿Qué le daré? (poner la mano bajo la barbilla, pensando.)

Comenzó a caminar para ver qué podía hallar. Caminó hasta que encontró una gallina. "Buenos días, (saludar con la cabeza) señora gallina," dijo Daniel. "¿Me puede dar algo para el compleaños de mi mamá?" "Cluck, cluck," contestó la gallina, "le puedo dar un huevo." "Gracias," dijo Daniel con voz triste, "pero ella ya tiene un huevo." "Vamos a ver que podemos encontrar," dijo la gallina.

Daniel y la gallina se fueron caminando y caminaron hasta que encontraron una gansa. "Buenos días, señora gansa," dijo Daniel. "¿Me puede dar algo para el compleaños de mi mamá?" "Honk, honk," dijo la señora gansa. "Le puedo dar plumas para hacer una almohada." "Gracias," dijo Daniel, "pero ella ya tiene una almohada." "Vamos a ver qué podemos encontrar," dijo la señora gansa.

Daniel, la gallina y la gansa se fueron caminando y caminaron hasta que encontraron una chiva. "Buenos días, señora chiva," dijo Daniel. "¿Me puede dar algo para el cumpleaños de mi mamá?" "Maa, maa," dijo la chiva. "Le puedo dar leche para hacer queso." "Gracias," (tristemente) dijo Daniel, "pero ella ya tiene queso." "Vamos a ver que podemos encontrar," dijo la chiva.

Daniel, la gallina, la gansa y la chiva caminaron y caminaron hasta que encontraron una borrega. "Buenos días, señora borrega," dijo Daniel. "¿Me puede dar algo para el cumpleaños de mi mamá?" "Baa, baa," dijo la borrega. "Le puedo dar lana para hacer una cobija calientita." "Gracias," (tristemente) dijo Daniel, "pero ella ya tiene una cobija." "Vamos a ver que podemos encontrar," dijo la borrega.

Daniel, la gallina, la gansa, la chiva y la borrega caminaron y caminaron hasta que encontraron una vaca. "Buenos días, señora vaca," dijo Daniel. "¿Me puede dar algo para el cumpleaños de mi mamá?" "Le puedo dar leche y crema," dijo la vaca. "Gracias," (tristemente) dijo Daniel, "pero ella ya tiene leche y crema." "Entonces pregúntele al señor oso que vive arriba de esa loma," dijo la vaca. "Bueno," dijo Daniel, "vamos a preguntarle al señor oso." "No," dijo la gallina. "No," dijo la gansa. "No," dijo la chiva. "No," dijo la borrega. "No, No, No," dijo la vaca. Y Daniel tuvo que ir solito a buscar al señor oso.

Corrió y corrió hasta que llegó a la loma. Caminó y caminó hasta que llegó al bosque donde había muchos árboles. Allí se encontró al señor oso.

"Buenos días, señor oso," dijo Daniel. "¿Me puede dar algo para el cumpleaños de mi mamá?" "Hmmm, hmmm," murmuró el oso. "Yo no tengo nada que darle pero puedo sugerir que le puedes dar." Entonces el oso se acercó y le dijo algo en el oído. Daniel le dió las gracias y corrió por el bosque. Bajó la loma corriendo hasta que llegó a su casa.

"¡Adivina que te voy a dar para tu cumpleaños!" le dijo a su mamá. Su mamá se puso a adivinar. "¿Es un huevo?" le preguntó. "No, no es un huevo," dijo Daniel. "¿Es una almohada?" preguntó la mamá. "No, no es una almohada," dijo Daniel. "¿Es queso?" preguntó la mamá. "No, no es queso," dijo Daniel. "¿Es una cobija?" preguntó la mamá. "No, no es una cobija," dijo Daniel. "¿Es leche o crema?" preguntó la mamá. "No, no es leche o crema," dijo Daniel. "No puedo adivinar, mi hijito," dijo la mamá. "¿Qué es lo que me vas a dar?" "Esto," dijo Daniel y se acercó a su mamá y con sus dos brazitos le dió un abrazo tan fuerte como el de un oso. Esto hizo a su mamá muy feliz.

GLOSSARY

KEY

adj.	-	adjective
adv.	-	adverb
conj.	-	conjunction
def. art.	-	definite article
dem. pron.	-	demonstrative pronoun
indef. art.	-	indefinite article
interj.	-	interjection
n.f.	-	feminine noun
n.m.	-	masculine noun
prep.	-	preposition
pron.	-	pronoun
p.p.	-	past participle
rel. adj.	-	relative adjective
rel. pron.	-	relative pronoun
v.i.	-	intransitive verb
v.t.	-	transitive verb

SPANISH-ENGLISH VOCABULARY

a

a - (prep) to, at

a menudo - (adv) often

abajo - (adv) down, below

abeja - (nf) bee

abrigo - (nm) overcoat

abril - (nm) April

abrir - (vt) to open

abuelo - (nm) grandfather

acá - (adv) here, over here

acabar - (vt) to finish, to end

acaso - (adv) perhaps, maybe

acceso - (nm) access

aceite - (nm) oil

acera - (nf) sidewalk

acerca de - (prep) about, concerning

acompañar - (vt) to accompany

aconsejar - (vt) to advise

actividad - (nf) activity

acuario - (nm) aquarium

además - (adv) furthermore, beside

adentro - (adv) within

adiós - (interj) goodbye

adivinar - (vt) to guess

adonde - (adv) where

adornar - (vt) to adorn

afirmar - (vt) to affirm, declare

afuera - (adv) outside, out

agosto - (nm) August

agua - (nf) water, rain

agüero - (nm) omen

aguijón - (nm) sting

águila - (nf) eagle

agujero - (nm) hole

ahora - (adv) now

aire - (nm) air, wind, breeze

al azar - (adv) at random

alacrán - (nm) scorpion

alargado - (pp) lengthened, elongated

ala - (nf) wing

alegre - (adj) gay, happy

alegría - (nf) cheer, happiness

alfombra - (nf) carpet, rug

alguno - (adj) some, any; (pron) someone, something

alimentar - (vt) to feed

alimento - (nm) food

aliviar - (vt) to relieve

almohada - (nf) pillow

almorzar - (vi) to eat lunch

almuerzo - (nm) lunch

alrededor - (adv) around	*árbol* - (nm) tree
alto - (adj) high, tall	*arbusto* - (nm) shrub
aluminio - aluminum	*arco iris* - (nm) rainbow
alumno - (nm-f) pupil	*ardilla* - (nf) squirrel
alzar - (vt) to raise	*aritmética* - (nf) arithmetic
amarillo - (adj) yellow	*arrastrarse* - (vr) to crawl
amigo - (nm) friend	*arreglar* - (vt) to arrange
añadir - (vt) to add	*¡arre!* - (interj) giddap!
análogo - (adj) analagous	*arriba* - (adv) above, up
anaranjado - (adj) orange colored	*arroz* - (nm) rice
anciano - (adj) old; (nm) old man	*artículo* - (nm) article
ancho - (adj) wide, broad	*así* - (adv) so, thus
andar - (vi) to walk, to move	*asistente* - (nm) assistant, helper
animal - (nm-adj) animal	*asociar* - (vt) to associate, to attach
antes - (adv) formerly; (adj) previous	*áspero* - (adj) rough, hard
año - (nm) year	*atención* - (nf) attention
apagar - (vt) to turn off, to put out	*atrás* - (adv) back, behind, ago
apenas - (adv) scarcely, hardly, barely	*aula* - (nf) classroom
apellido - (nm) surname, family name	*autobús* - (nm) bus
apio - (nm) celery	*ave* - (nf) bird
aprender - (vt-i) to learn	*avena* - (nf) oats, oatmeal
aprender de memoria - to learn by heart	*avión* - (nm) airplane
aproximar - (vt) to approach	*ayuda* - (nm) help
aquel - (dem pron m) that, that one	*ayudar* - (vt-i) to help
aquí - (adv) here	*azar* - (nm) hazard, chance
araña - (nf) spider	*azúcar* - (nm-f) sugar
	azul - (adj-nm) blue

b

bacalao - (nm) codfish

bailar - (vt-i) to dance

bajar - (vi) to descent

bajo (bajito) - (adj) short, soft

balar - (vi) to bleat

balón - (nm) balloon, large ball

banco - (nm) bench, bank

bandeja - (nf) tray

bandera - (nf) flag, banner

bañar - (vt) to bathe, to wash

baño - (nm) bath, bathroom

banqueta - (nf) sidewalk (Mex)

barco - (nm) boat, ship

barrera - (nf) barrier, fence

barrio - (nm) district (of a city)

bastante - (adj-adv) enough

basura - (nf) trash, garbage

basurero - (nm) garbage collector

bebé - (nm) baby

bebida - (nf) drink

bello - (adj) beautiful

bellota - (nf) acorn

beso - (nm) kiss

betabeles - (nm) beets

biblioteca - (nf) library

bicicleta - (nf) bicycle

bien - (adv) well, all right, OK

bigotes - (nm) mustache

blanco - (adj) white; (nm) white person

blando - (adj) bland, soft, weak

bloque - (nm) block

blusa - (nf) blouse

boca - (nf) mouth

bola - (nf) ball, sphere

boloña - (nf) bologna

bollito - (nm) muffin, roll

bombero - (nm) fireman

bonito - (adj) pretty

borrador - (nm) eraser

borrego - (nm) lamb, "dunce" (colloq)

bostezo - (nm) yawn

bote - (nm) boat

botón - (nm) button

bravo - (adj) brave, wild, fierce

brazo - (nm) arm, foreleg of an animal

brillar - (vi) to shine

brisa - (nf) breeze

broma - (nf) joke, disappointment

bruja - (nf) witch

bueno - (adj) good, kind; (adv) very well

buenos días - (idiom) good day

buho - (nm) owl

burro - (nm) donkey

buscar - (vt) to look for, to seek

C

caballo - (nm) horse

cabeza - (nf) head, leader

cabra - (nf) goat

cacerola - (nf) saucepan

cacto - (nm) cactus

cada - (adj) each, every

caer - (vi) to fall, to drop

café- (nm) coffee, cafe

cafetería - (nf) cafeteria

caja - (nf) box

calabaza - (nf) pumpkin, gourd

calcetín - (nm) sock

calcio - (nm) calcium

caldo - (nm) broth, salad dressing

calentar - (vt) to warm; to heat

calor - (nm) heat; warmth

cama - (nf) bed

cambiar - (vt or i) to change, to
        exchange

cambio - (nm) change

caminar - (vi or t) to go; to walk

camino - (nm) way, road

camote - (nm) sweet potato

campo - (nm) country

canario - (nm) canary

canasta - (nf) basket

cantar - (vt or i) to sing

cantidad - (nf) quantity

canto - (nm) song, epic poem

caparazón - (nm) shell of insects

cara - (nf) face, expression

caracol - (nm) snail; sea shell

¡caramba! - (interj) darn it! gracious!

carbón - (nm) coal

carga - (nf) load, burden

carne - (nf) meat, flesh

carne asada - (nf) roast meat

carne guisada - (nf) stewed meat

carne picada - (nf) chopped meat

carro - (nm) car, wagon

carta - (nf) letter; chart; mop

cartero - (nm) postman; mailman

casa - (nf) house, home

cáscara - (nf) shell, rind, bush

cascarón - (nm) egg shell

cavidad - (nf) cavity

cebolla - (nf) onion

cemento - (nm) cement

cena - (nf) supper

centro - (nm) center, middle

cepillar - (vt) to brush

cepillo - (nm) brush

cerca - (adv) near, close

cercar - (vt) to encircle, to enclose

cereal - (nm or adj) cereal

cereza - (nf) cherry

cerdo - (nm) hog, pig

cero - (nm) zero

césped - (nm) lawn, grass

cesta - (nf) basket, wastebasket

ciencia - (nf) science, knowledge

ciento - (adj or nm) hundred

cierto - (adj) certain, sure;
(adv) surely

cifra - (nf) number

cinco - (adj or nm) five

cintura - (nf) waist

circo - (nm) circus

circulación - (nf) circulation, traffic

círculo - (nm) circle, club

ciruela - (nf) plum, prune

ciudad - (nf) city

clarín - (nm) bugle

claro - (adj) clear; bright, light (of
colors); skin or weave (of
liquids, hair, etc.)

clase - (nf) class, class of students;
kind, sort

clasificar - (vt) to classify, arrange

clavel - (nm) carnation

clérigo - (nm) clergyman

clima - (nm) climate; weather

clínica - (nf) clinic

cobre - (nm) copper

coche - (nm) car

cocina - (nf) kitchen, stove

cocinar - (vi or t) to cook; to bake

col - (nf) cabbage

cola - (nf) tail; *(hacer cola)* to
stand in line

colección - (nf) collection

colgar - (vt) to hang

coliflor - (nf) cauliflower

colina - (nf) hill

colmillo - (nm) eyetooth, canine tooth

colocar - (vt) to arrange, to place

color - (nm) color

color de café - (adj) brown

colorado - (adj) red, reddish; "embarrasse

colorar - (vt) to color, to paint

columpio - (nm) seesaw

comenzar - (vt or i) to begin

comer - (vt) to eat

comida - (nf) food; dinner

como - (adv or conj) how; as (in comparison)

¿cómo no? - (interr) why not?

comparación - (nf) comfortable, comparison

comparar - (vt) to compare

complementario - (adj) complementary

complemento - (nm) complement; (gram-
          object)

completar - (vt) to complete, finish

comprar - (vt) to buy; (vi) to shop

comprender - (vt) to understand

comprobar - (vt) to verify, to check

común - (adj) common, usual

comunidad - (nf) community

con - (prep) with

concha - (nf) shell; sea shell

conclusión - - (nf) conclusion

concreto - (adj) concrete, real

conejo - (nm) rabbit

conjunto - (nm) set (math) whole,
          entirely

cono - (nm) cone

conocer - (vt) to know

conserje - (nm) janitor

constar de - (vi) to consist of

construir - (vt) to build, to form

contar - (vt) to tell; relate

contener - (vt) to contain

contenido - (nm) contents

contento - (adj) glad, happy, pleased

convenir - (vi) to agree; to be suitable

convertir - (vt) to convert

corazón - (nm) heart

corral - (nm) corral, barnyard

corregir - (vt) to correct

correo - (nm) mail

correr - (vt or i) to run

correspondencia - (nf) correspondence,
          mail

cortada - (nf) cut, slash

cortar - (vt) to cut, to cut out

corto - (adj) short; bashful

cosa - (nf) thing; matter

crecer - (vi) to grow; to increase

creyón - (nm) crayon

cruz - (nf) cross; plus sign (math)

cruzar - (vt) to cross

cuaderno - (nm) notebook

cuadrado - (adj or nm) square

cuadro - (nm) picture, square

cual - (rel & indef adj & pron) which

cuando - (adv & conj) when

cuantos - (rel adj & pron) as much as,
          as many as

cuarto - (nm) room

cuarto de baño - (nm) bathroom)

cuatro - (adj or nm) four

cubo - (nm) cube

cubrir - (vt) to cover

cuchara - (nf) spoon, tablespoon

cucharada - (nf) tablespoonful

cucharita - (nf) teaspoon

cuchillo - (nm) knife

cuello - (nm) neck, collar (of a shirt)

cuento - (nm) story, tale

cuerda - (nf) cord; rope; string

cuerno - (nm) horn

cuerpo - (nm) body

cuidado - (nm) care, attention

cuidar - (vt) to look after; to take care of

cumpleaños - (nm) birthday (s & pl)

curita - (nf) bandaid

curso - (nm) course; school year

curva - (nf) curve; bend

<u>ch</u>

chica - (nf) little girl

chicle - (nm) chewing gum

chile - (nm) chili

chiquito - (adj) small, tiny; (nm) little boy

chiste - (nm) joke

chistoso - (adj) funny, humorous, witty

chocolate - (nm) chocolate

chorizo - (nm) sausage

chuleta - (nf) cutlet, chop

d

dar - (vt) to give

de - (prep) of, from, by

deber - (vt) to owe; (aux verb) ought to, must

decidir - (vt) to decide

decir - (vt) to say, to speak

dedo - (nm) finger, toe

deducir - (vt) to deduce, infer

defender - (vt) to defend; to protect

definido - (adj) definite, defined

delgado - (adj) thin

demasiado - (adj) too much; (adv) too

demostrar - (vt) to show, prove

dentista - (nm or f) dentist

dentro - (adv) inside

dependiente - (nm or f) salesclerk

derecho - (adj) right, straight

desayunar - (vi) to eat breakfast

desayuno - (nm) breakfast

descansar - (vi) to rest, relax

descubrimiento - (nm) discovery

desear - (vt) to desire; to want

desgarrar - (vt) to tear, to rend

designar - (vt) to designate

desigual - (adj) dissimilar; unequal

desigualdad - (nf) inequality

después - (adv) after

destreza - (nf) skill

determinado - (adj) determined; definite; specific

día - (nm) day, daylight

día despejado - clear, bright day

dibujar - (vt) to draw

dibujo - (nm) drawing

diciembre - (nm) December

diente - (nm) tooth

diez - (adj & nm) ten

diferencia - (nf) difference

diferente - (adj) different

digestión - (nf) digestion

dinero - (nm) money

director - (nm) director

disco - (nm) record

diseño - (nm) design; drawing

disfraz - (nm) disguise

dispensar - (vt) to excuse, absolve

distancia - (nf) distance

distinguir - (vt) to distinguish

distinto - (adj) distinct, different

diverso - (adj) diverse

divertirse - (vr) to enjoy oneself; to have a good time

doctor - (nm) doctor

dolor - (nm) pain

doméstico - (adj & nm) domestic

domingo - (nm) Sunday

dónde - (rel adv) where; (prep) at, in

dorado - (adj) gilded; golden

dormir - (vi) to sleep

dos - (adj & nm) two

duende - (nm) goblin, fairy

dulce - (adj) sweet; (nm) candy

durante - (prep) during

durazno - (nm) peach

duro - (adj) hard, harsh; (adv) hard

e

ejemplo - (nm) example, pattern

ejercicio - (nm) exercise, practice

ejote - (nm) green bean (Mex)

el - (def art) the, the one

él - (pron) he; (obj of prep) him

elección - (nf) election; choice

elefante - (nm or f) elephant

elegir - (vt) to elect, to choose

elemento - (nm) element

elevado - (adj) elevated

elote - (nm) ear of corn

ella - (pron) she; (obj of prep) her

ellos - (pron) they, you (plural)

empezar - (vt) to begin

emplear - (vt) to employ, to use

en - (prep) in, into, on, at

enano - (nm) dwarf

en casa - (prep) at home

en seguida - (adv) immediately

encima - (adv) over, above

encontrar - (vt or i) to meet, to come upon

enero - (nm) January

enfadado - (adj) angry, furious

enfermera - (nf) nurse

enojado - (adj) angry, annoyed

ensalada - (nf) salad

enseñanza - (nf) teaching

enseñar - (nt) to teach; to show

entender - (vt or i) to understand

entonces - (adv) then

entre - (prep) among, between

escalera - (nf) staircase; stairs

escama - (nf) scale (of fish, reptiles)

escaso - (adj) small, scarce

escolar - (adj) scholastic; (nm) student

esconder - (vt) to hide, to conceal

escorpión - (nm) scorpion

escribir - (vt) to write

escuela - (nf) school

ese - (dem adj) that (m)

esfera - (nf) sphere

esófago - (nm) esophagus

espacio - (nm) space

espalda - (nf) back (of a person)

especie - (nf) species, kind

espejo - (nm) mirror

espejuelos - (nm pl) eyeglasses

esperanza - (nf) hope

esperar - (vt) to wait for, to hope for

espiga - (nf) ear (of grain)

espinaca - (nf) spinach

espíritu - (nm) spirit

esposa - (nf) wife

esquema - (nm) outline, sketch

estaca - (nf) stake; stick

estación - (nf) station; season

estar - (vi) to be

este - (nm) east; (dem adj) this

estropeado - (adj) spoiled; damaged

estómago - (nm) stomach

estornudar - (vi) to sneeze

estrecho - (adj) narrow; snug

estrella - (nf) star

estudiante - (nf or f) student

estudiar - (vt) to study

estufa - (nf) stove

etiqueta - (nf) etiquette; formality

excepto - (adv) except

excusado - (nm) toilet

exigir - (vt) to demand; to require

extranjero - (nm or adj) foreign, alien

extraño - (adj) strange

f

fabricar - (vt) to build; to manufacture

fachada - (nf) facada, title page, appearance

falda - (nf) skirt

faltar - (vi) to be lacking, to fail

familia - (nf) family

familiar - (adj) familiar; familial

familiarizar - (vt) to familiarize

famoso - (adj) famous

farmacéutico - (nm) pharmacist

fatiga - (nf) fatigue; hardship

favor - (nm) favor

febrero - (nm) February

felicidad - (nf) happiness

feliz - (adj) happy

festejar - (vt) to entertain; to celebrate

ficha - (nf) index card, card file

fideo - (nm) spaghetti

fiebre - (nf) fever

fiera - (nf) wild beast

fiesta - (nf) party; holiday

figura - (nf) figure; shape

fila - (nf) file, row, line

fin - (nm) end

flaco - (adj) thin, weak

flan - (nm) custard

flanelógrafo - (nm) flannel board

flauta - (nf) flute

flecha - (nf) arrow

floja - (adj) loose; lazy

flor - (nf) flower

foca - (nf) seal

fonógrafo - (nm) phonograph, record player

forma - (nf) form; shape; manner

formar - (vt) to form, to shape

fracaso - (nm) failure

frase - (nf) sentence; phrase

fregar - (vt) to scrub, to wash (dishes)

fresa - (nf) strawberry

frijol - (nm) bean

frío - (adj) cold; (nm) cold, chill

frito - (adj) fried

fruta - (nf) fruit

fuego - (nm) fire

fuente - (nf) fountain

fuerza - (nf) strength; force

g

gafas - (nf pl) spectacles

galleta - (nf) cracker

gallina - (nf) hen; chicken

gallo - (nm) rooster; cock

ganar - (vt) to gain, to win, to earn

garaje - (nm) garage

garbanzo - (nm) chick pea

garra - (nf) claw

gasolina - (nf) gasoline

gato - (nm) cat

gelatina - (nf) gelatin

gente - (nf) people, folk

gerente - (nm) manager

gigante - (nm) giant

gis - (nm) crayon

golosina - (nf) delicacy; sweet tidbit

goma - (nf) gum, rubber, rubber band

gordo - (adj) fat, plump; (nm) fat person

gorra - (nf) cap

gota - (nf) drop

gotear - (vt) to drip; leak

gozar - (vt) to enjoy; derive pleasure from

grabadora - (nf) recorder

gracias - (nf pl) thanks

grama - (nf) grass (P.R.)

grande - (adj) large; great

granero - (nm) barn

granja - (nf) farm

grano - (nm) grain; pimple

graznar - (vi) to croak; to caw

grillo - (nm) cricket

gris - (adj & nm) gray

grupo - (nm) group

guajolote - (nm) turkey (Mex.)

guante - (nm) glove

guardar - (vt) to hold, to keep, to save

guitarra - (nf) guitar

gusano - (nm) worm

gustar - (vt) to taste; (vi) to please, to be liked

gusto - (nm) taste; liking, pleasure

h

haber - (vt) to have, to own

habichuela verde - (nf) string bean

hacer - (vt) to do; to make

hacia - (prep) toward; near; about

hallar - (vt) to find; come upon

harina - (nf) flour

hasta - (prep) until; as far as

hay - (adv expression) there is; there are

helado - (adj) frozen; (nm) ice cream

helecho - (nm) fern

hermano - (nm) brother

hierba - (nf) grass

hierro - (nm) iron

hígado - (nm) liver

hija - (nf) daughter

hijo - (nm) son

historia - (nf) history, story

hogar - (nm) home; fireplace

hoja - (nf) leaf; sheet (of paper)

hombre - (nm) man

hora - (nf) hour; time

hoy - (adv) today; at the present time

hueco - (nm) hole

hueso - (nm) bone; pit (of fruit)

huevo - (nm) egg

húmedo - (adj) humid, moist

i

idéntico - (adj) identical

igual - (adj) equal, even

imaginar - (vt) to imagine

imán - (nm) magnet

imitar - (vt) to imitate

incendio - (nm) fire

indio - (adj or nm) Indian

individual - (adj) individual

informar - (vt) to inform

inglés - (adj) English; (nm) Englishman

instrumento - (nm) instrument

interés - (nm) interest

interesante - (adj) interesting

intestino - (adj) intestinal

interpretar - (vt) to interpret

inventar - (vt) to invent

invierno - (nm) winter

ir - (vt) to go

izquierdo - (adj) left

j

jabón - (nm) soap

jalea - (nf) jelly

jamás - (adv) never

jardín - (nm) garden

jarro - (nm) pitcher, jug

jaula - (nf) cage

jota - (nf) the letter "j"

joven - (adj) young; (nm) young person

juego - (nm) game

jugar - (vi) to play, (vt) to play at

jugo - (nm) juice

juguete - (nm) toy; plaything

julio - (nm) July

junio - (nm) June

juntar - (vt) to join; to unite; place together

junto - (adj) joined; united

justo - (adj) just; correct, exact

labio - (nm) lip

lado - (nm) side; direction

ladrar - (vi) to bark

lago - (nm) lake

laguna - (nf) lagoon; pond

lámina - (nf) picture (in a book)

lámpara - (nf) lamp

lana - (nf) wool

lápiz - (nm) pencil

largo - (adj) long

lástima - (nf) pity; compassion

latino - (adj & nm) Latin

lavamanos - (nm pl) washstand

lavar - (vt) to wash

lazo - (nm) bow; lasso

leche - (nf) milk

lechero - (nm) milkman

lechuga - (nf) lettuce

leer - (vt) to read

legumbre - (nf) vegetable

lejos - (adv) far; far off

lente de aumento - (nm) magnifying glass

lenteja - (nf) lentil

lentes - (nm pl) eyeglasses

león - (nm) lion

letra - (nf) letter; handwriting

levantarse - (vr) to rise; to get up

libro - (nm) book

ligar - (vt) to bind; to tie

limón - (nm) lemon

limonada - (nf) lemonade

lindo - (adj) pretty

línea - (nf) line

liso - (adj) smooth

listo - (adj) with *estar* - ready;
with *ser* - clever

lista - (nf) list; roll

lodo - (nm) mud

loma - (nf) hill, slope

lomo - (nm) back (of an animal)

lombriz - (nf) earthworm

los - (def art pl) the

luego - (adv) immediately; soon; then

lugar - (nm) place

luna - (nf) moon

lunes - (nm s & pl) Monday

luz - (nf) light

ll

llamar - (vt) to call

llano - (nm) plain, flat ground;
(adj) plain, even

llanto - (nm) weeping, crying

llanura - (nf) plain; prairie

llegar - (vi) to arrive; to come;
to reach; to attain

llenar - (vt) to fill; to satisfy

llevar - (vt) to carry; to wear

llover - (v impers) to rain; to pour

lluvia - (nf) rain, flood

lluvioso - (adj) rainy

m

machacar - (vt) to crush

madera - (nf) wood

madre - (nf) mother

maestro(a) - (nm or f) teacher

magnífico - (adj) magnificent

maíz - (nm) corn

mal - (nm) evil, harm; (adv) badly, bad, poorly

mamá - (nf) mother

mamar - (vt) to suck

manada - (nf) herd

manchar - (vt) to spot, stain

manera - (nf) manner, way

mano - (nf) hand, "pal" (slang)

manso - (adj) meek, gentle

manta - (nf) blanket

manteca - (nf) lard; grease

mantequilla - (nf) butter

manzana - (nf) apple; city block

mañana - (nf) morning

mapa - (nm) map

máquina de cortar zacate - (nf) lawnmower

mar - (nm or f) sea

marcar - (vt) to brand; to point out; to dial (telephone)

margarita - (nf) daisy

mariposa - (nf) butterfly

martes - (nm) Tuesday

marzo - (nm) March

más - (adv) more, plus, longer, besides

más o menos - more or less

masa - (nf) mass

máscara - (nf) mask, disguise

masticar - (vt) to chew

matemáticas - (nf) mathematics

mayo - (nm) May

mayor - (adj) greater, larger, older

mazorca - (nf) ear of corn

mecedora - (nf) rocking chair

mediante - (prep) by means of

medicina - (nf) medicine

médico - (nm) physician

medida - (nf) measure

medio - (adj & adv) half; (adj) middle

mediodía - (nm) noon

mejor - (adj) better

melón - (nm) melon

menor - (adj) smaller, younger; (nm) minor

menos - (adv) less; minus, except

mentira - (nf) lie

mercado - (nm) market

mercancía - (nf) merchandise

merienda - (nf) snack; picnic

mes - (nm) month

mesa - (nf) table, desk

meter - (vt) to put in; insert

mezclar - (vt) to mix

mi - (poss adj) my

miedo - (nm) fear

miel - (nf) honey

mientras - (conj) while; as; whereas

miércoles - (nm) Wednesday

mina - (nf) mine; lead (of a pencil)

mineral - (adj & nm) mineral

minuto - (adj) minute

mirar - (vt) to look at; to watch

mismo - (adj & pron) same

moderno - (adj & nm) modern

molino - (nm) mill

moneda - (nf) coin, money

mono - (adj) nice, cute

montaña - (nf) mountain

montar - (vi) to mount; to get on; to ride

monte - (nm) mountain

morado - (adj & nm) purple

moreno - (adj) brown; brunette

morir - (vi) to die

mosca - (nf) fly

mostrar - (vt) show, point out

mover - (vt) to move; to persuade

movimiento - (nm) movement; motion

muchacho - (nm) boy

mucho - (adj, adv & pron) much, very much

muela - (nf) molar

mugir - (vi) to moo

muñeca - (nf) wrist; doll

murciélago - (nm) bat (animal)

museo - (nm) museum

música - (nf) music

muy - (adv) very, greatly, most

n

nacer - (vi) to be born; to emerge

nada - (indef. pron) nothing

nadar - (vi) to swim

nadie - (indef pron) nobody; no one

naranja - (nf) orange

nariz - (nf) nose

natural - (adj)natural; native

naturaleza - (nf) nature

Navidad - (nf) Christmas

necesario - (adj) necessary

necesitar - (vt) to need

negro - (adj & nm) black; negro

nene - (nm) baby; child

nido - (nm) nest

nieve - (nf) snow; sherbert

ninguno - (adj) not any; (pron) no one

niño - (nm) child

no - (adv) no, not

noche - (nf) night

nombre - (nm) name, noun

normal - (adj) normal

norte - (adj & nm) north

nosotros - (pers pron) we, us

noviembre - (nm) November

nube - (nf) cloud

nubloso - (adj) cloudy

nuestro - (poss adj & pron) our, ours

nuevo - (adj) new

numeración - (nf) numbering

número - (nm) number, numeral

nunca - (adv) never

O

o - (conj) or, either

objeto - (nm) object

observar - (vt) to observe

obtener - (vt) to get, to obtain

ocho - (adj & nm) eight

octubre - (nm) October

odio - (nm) hate; hatred

oeste - (nm) west

oficina - (nf) office

oído - (nm) ear; hearing

oír - (vt or i) to hear; to listen

ojo - (nm) eye

olfato - (nm) sense of smell

olor - (nm) odor

operación - (nf) operation

oración - (nf) speech; prayer

orden - (nm) order; arrangement

ordenar - (vt) to order; command; arrange

oreja - (nf) ear, outer ear

oro - (nm) gold

oscuridad - (nf) darkness; obscurity

oso - (nm) bear

otoño - (nm) autumn, fall

otra vez - (adv) again

otro - (adj & pron) another

oveja - (nf) sheep

oxígeno - (nm) oxygen

padre - (nm) father

padres - (nm pl) parents

página - (nf) page

país - (nm) country

pájaro - (nm) bird

pálido - (adj) pale

palma - (nf) palm tree

palo - (nm) stick

paloma - (nf) dove, pigeon

pan - (nm) bread

panadero - (nm) baker

pantalones - (nm) trousers

pañuelo - (nm) handkerchief

papá- (nm) papa, dad

papa - (nf) potato

papel - (nm) paper; part

paquete - (nm) package

par - (adj) equal; (nm) pair

para - (prep) for, toward, in order to

paraguas - (nm) umbrella

parecer - (vi) to appear, seem

parecido - (adj) like, alike, similar

pared - (nf) wall

pareja - (nf) pair, couple

P

pariente - (nm) relative

parque - (nm) park

parte - (nf) part

Pascua Florida - (nf) Easter

paso - (nm) step

pasta - (nf) paste; batter

pastel - (nm) pie, pastry, tart

pata - (nf) leg or paw of an animal

patio - (nm) patio, courtyard

patio de recreo - (nm) playground

pato - (nm) duck

patrulla - (nf) patrol; gang

payaso - (nm) clown

pecho - (nm) chest, breast

pedazo - (nm) piece

pedir - (vt) to request, to ask

pegadura - (nf) pasting, adhesion

pegar - (vt) to paste, to glue; to strike

pelo - (nm) hair

pelota - (nf) ball

pensamiento - (nm) thought

pensar - (vt & i) to think

peor - (adj & adv) worse; worst

pepino - (nm) cucumber

pequeño - (adj) small; (nm) child

pera - (nf) pear

perdido - (adj) lost

perdón - (nm) pardon; forgiveness

peregrino - (adj) migratory;
    (n.m.) pilgrim

periquito - (nm) parakeet

permiso - (nm) permission

permitir - (vt) to allow, to permit

pero - (conj) but, except; yet

perro - (nm) dog

persona - (nf) person

personaje - (nm) character (in a story)

pertenecer - (vi) to belong, to pertain

pesado - (adj) heavy, tiresome;
    (nm) bore

pesar - (vt or i) to weigh

pescado - (nm) fish (edible)

pescar - (vt or i) to fish

peso - (nm) weight; peso

petróleo - (nm) petroleum; oil

pez - (nm) fish

picar - (vt) to prick, to puncture

pico - (nm) beak

pie - (nm) foot

piedra - (nf) stone

piel - (nf) skin, hide

pierna - (nf) leg

pintar - (vt) to paint

pintura - (nf) paint; painting

piña - (nf) pine cone; pineapple

piojo - (nm) louse

pipa - (nf) smoking pipe

piso - (nm) floor; story (of a
    building

pizarra - (nf) blackboard

pizarrón - (nm) blackboard

planta - (nf) plant; sole of a foot

plátano - (nm) banana

platicar - (vi) to chat

plata - (nf) silver; money

plato - (nm) plate; dish

playa - (nf) beach; shore

pluma - (nf) pen; feather

pobre - (adj) poor; (nm) poor person

poco - (adj) a little; not much

poder - (vi) to be able

poema - (nm) poem

policía - (nf) police; policeman

pollo - (nm) chicken

ponche - (nm) punch (drink)

poner - (vt) to put, to place, to set

poner la mesa - (vt) to set the table

ponerse - (vt) to become; to put on

ponerse de pie - (vr) to stand up

ponerse en línea - (vr) to get in line

por - (prep) by, by way of; through

por favor - (interj) please

porque - (conj) because; so that

porqué - (nm) reason, motive, cause

portada - (nf) cover (of a book)

portarse - (vr) to behave

posibilidad - (nf) possibility

posible - (adj) possible

preciso - (adj) necessary; exact

preguntar - (vt) to ask; to question

preparar - (vt) to prepare

presentar - (vt) to present

prestar atención - (vt) to pay attention

primavera - (nf) spring

primero - (adj, adv, nm) first

primo - (nm) cousin

principio - (nm) beginning; principle

prisma - (nm) prism

problema - (nm) problem

profesor - (nm) professor; teacher

progresar - (vi) to progress

progresión - (nf) progression

progreso - (nm) progress

pronto - (adj) prompt; ready

propiedad - (nf) property; ownership

proteger - (vt) to protect

próximo - (adj) next; close; near

púa - (nf) quill, spine, prickle

pueblo - (nm) town

puerco - (nm) pig

puerco-espín - (nm) porcupine

puerta - (nf) door

puerto - (nm) port, harbor

pues - (conj) for, since, because, then

pulga - (nf) flee

pulgada - (nf) inch

pulgar - (nm) thumb

que - (rel pro) who, whom, that which   *9*

qué - (inter adj & pro) which, what

quebrar - (vt & i) to break

quedar - (vi) to remain, to stay

quemar - (vt & i) to burn

querer - (vt & i) to want, to wish, to love

querido - (adj) dear; (nm) beloved, lover

queso - (nm) cheese

quien - (rel pron) who, whom

quitar - (vt) to remove; to take away

quitarse - (vr) to take off (clothing)

quizás - (adv) maybe, perhaps

rábano - (nm) radish

rabo - (nm) tail

raíz - (nf) root

ramo - (nm) small branch

rana - (nf) frog

rápido - (adj) quick, swift

rato - (nm) moment, while, period of time

ratón - (nm) mouse

rayo - (nm) ray, beam

rebuznar - (vi) to bray

recámara - (nf) bedroom (Mex)

receta - (nf) prescription, recipe

recibir - (vt) to receive; to greet

recitar - (vt & i) to recite

recoger - (vt) to gather, to pick up; to get back

recomendar - (vt) to recommend, advise

reconocer - (vt) to recognize

recortar - (vt) to cut out

recrear - (vt) to amuse; to delight

rectangular - (adj) rectangular

rectángulo - (nm) rectangle

redondear - (vt) to round; round off

redondo - (adj) round

referir - (vt) to refer

refresco - (nm) refreshment

refrigeradora - (nf) refrigerator

regalar - (vt) to give; to present

regalo - (nm) present; gift

regazo - (nm) lap

regla - (nf) rule; ruler

regresar - (vi) to return

reír - (vi) to laugh, (vt) to laugh at

relación - (nf) relation; report

relinchar - (vi) to neigh; whinny

reloj - (nm) clock; watch

repasar - (vt) to review

repaso - (nm) review

repetir - (vt) to repeat

repollo - (nm) cabbage

representación - (nf) representation

resolver - (vt) to solve; to resolve

restante - (nm) remainder

restar - (vt & i) to subtract

resto - (nm) rest; remainder

resultado - (nm) result

reunir - (vt) to reunite; to join

río - (nm) river

risa - (nf) laughter

roca - (nf) rock

rodear - (vi) to go around; (vt) to surround

rodeo - (nm) rodeo; turn; corral

rojo - (adj) red; reddish

rompecabezas - (nm) puzzle

ropa - (nf) clothes

ropero - (nm) clothier; clothes closet

rosado - (adj) rosy; pink

rubio - (adj) blond; (nm) a blond

rueda - (nf) wheel; circular arrangement

rugir - (vi) to roar; to rumble; to growl

ruido - (nm) noise; fuss

ruptura - (nf) rupture

ruta - (nf) route

S

sábado - (nm) Saturday

saber - (vt & i) to know, to know how
    to (+inf.)

sabroso - (adj) tasty, flavorful

sal - (nf) salt

sala - (nf) living room

sala de clase - (nf) classroom

salchicha - (nf) sausage

salero - (nm) salt shaker

salir - (vi) to go out; to leave

salpicar - (vt) to spatter; to splash

saltamontes - (nm) grasshopper

saltar - (vt & i) to jump; to leap

salud - (nf) health

salvaje - (adj) savage, wild;
    (nm) savage

sandía - (nf) watermelon

sapo - (nm) toad

seco - (adj) dry

según - (prep) according to

segundo - (adj & nm) second

seguridad - (nf) security; safety

seguro - (adj) safe, secure

seis - (adj & nm) six

semáforo - (nm) traffic light

semana - (nf) week

sembrar - (vt) to seed; plant; sow

semilla - (nf) seed

sentarse - (vr) to sit down

sentido - (nm) sense

sentir - (vt) to feel; to sense

señalar - (vt) point out

señor - (nm) Mr., sir

señora - (nf) Mrs., madam

señorita - (nf) Miss, young lady

separación - (nf) separation

separar - (vt) to separate

septiembre - (nm) September

ser - (vi) to be

ser vivo - (nm) human being

serie - (nf) series, sequence

servilleta - (nf) napkin

servir - (vt & i) to serve

sesión - (nf) session

seso - (nm) brain

seta - (nf) mushroom

sí - (conj) if, whether

siempre - (adv) always, ever; forever

siete - (adj & nm) seven

significado - (nm) meaning;
        (adj) important

significar - (vt) to signify; to mean

signo - (nm) sign; mark; symbol

silla - (nf) chair; saddle

símbolo - (nm) symbol; token

simpático - (adj) sympathetic, congenial, pleasant

simultáneo - (adj) simultaneous

sitio - (nm) place, location

situación - (nf) situation; position; condition

sobre - (prep & adv) over, above, on top of

sofá - (nm) sofa

sol - (nm) sun

solamente - (adv) only

solo - (adj) alone, only

solución - (nf) solution

sombra - (nf) shade, shadow

sombrero - (nm) hat

sopero - (nm) soup plate

sorpresa - (nf) surprise

su - (poss adj) his, her, yours, theirs, its

suave - (adj) soft, smooth, mild, gentle

sube y baja - (nm) seesaw

subir - (vt & i) to climb

sucio - (adj) dirty; soiled

suegra - (nf) mother-in-law

suegro - (nm) father-in-law

sumar - (vt & i) to add

suprimir - (vt) to suppress; to leave out

sur - (nm) south

t

tablero de noticias - (nm) bulletin board

tachar - (vt) to cross out

tacto - (nm) touch, sense of touch

tal - (adj) such, such a

tallo - (nm) stem; stalk

tamal - (nm) tamale

tamaño - (nm) size

también - (adv) also, too, as well

tanto - (adj & pron) so much, as much

tarjeta - (nf) card; label

taza - (nf) cup

tecolote - (nm) owl

tela de araña - (nf) spider web

teléfono - (nm) telephone

telescopio - (nm) telescope

televisión (nf); *televisor* (nm) - television set

tema - (nm) theme; subject

tenedor - (nm) fork

tener - (vt) to have; to hold

tercero - (adj & nm) third

terreno - (nm) terrain; ground

texto - (nm) text

tiempo - (nm) time; epoch

tienda - (nf) store

tierra - (nf) earth, land, soil

tijeras - (nf pl) scissors, shears

tinta - (nf) ink

tía - (nf) aunt

tío - (nm) uncle

tipo - (nm) type

títere - (nm) puppet

título - (nm) title; diploma

tiza - (nf) chalk

toalla de papel - (nm) paper towel

tocadiscos - (nm) record player

tocino - (nm) bacon

todavía - (adv) still, yet, even

todo - (adv) all, every

todo el mundo - (nm) everyone

tomar - (vt) to take; to drink

tomate - (nm) tomato

tonto - (adj) foolish; (nm) fool

tormenta - (nf) storm; misfortune

toronja - (nf) grapefruit

torta - (nf) cake; tart

tortilla - (nf) omelet; tortilla

tos - (nf) cough

tostada - (nf) toast

trabajar - (vt & i) to work

tractor - (nm) tractor

traer - (vt) to bring; to carry

tráfico - (nm) traffic

tragar - (vt) to swallow

tragedia - (nf) tragedy

traidor - (nm) traitor

tranquilo - (adj) tranquil, calm, easy going

trasladarse - (vr) to move; change residence

travieso - (adj) mischievous; naughty

trazo - (nm) line; trace; outline

trece - (adj & nm) thirteen

tren - (nm) train

tres - (adj & nm) three

triángulo - (nm) triangle

trigo - (nm) wheat

trinar - (vi) to trill; to warble

triste - (adj) sad; gloomy

trompeta - (nf) trumpet

tronco - (nm) trunk (of a tree)

trueno - (nm) thunder; thunderclap

tú - (poss adj) your

tulipán - (nm) tulip

u

último - (adj) last, final

un - (indef art) a, an, one

único - (adj) only, single, unique

unidad - (nf) unity; unit

unión - (nf) union, combination

unir - (vt) to connect, to join, to unite

uno - (indef pron) one, someone

urraca - (nf) magpie

usar - (vt) to use

usted - (pers pron) you, yourself

útil - (adj) useful; usable

utilizar - (vt) to utilize

uva - (nf) grape

V

vaca - (nf) cow

vacío - (adj) empty

vapor - (nm) vapor; steamboat

vaquero - (nm) cowboy

vara - (nf) rod, stick

variado - (adj) varied

variedad - (nf) variety

varios - (adj) several; various

vasija - (nf) vessel

vaso - (nm) glass; glassful

vecino - (nm) neighbor

vegetal- (nm) plant; vegetable

vehículo - (nm) vehicle

veinte - (adj & nm) twenty

vela - (nf) candle; sail; vigil

vendedor - (nm) seller, vendor

vender - (vt & i) to sell

venenoso - (adj) poisonous

venir - (vi) to come

ventana - (nf) window

ver - (vt & i) to see

verano - (nm) summer

verde - (adj) green

verdura - (nf) greenery; verdure

vergüenza - (nf) shame, modesty, embarrassment

vestido - (nm) dress, suit, clothes

vestirse - (vr) to dress oneself

vez - (nf) time; occasion; otra vez - again; tal vez - perhaps; a la vez - at the same time

viajar - (vt & i) to travel

viaje - (nm) trip

vicuña - (nf) vicuña

vida - (nf) life

vidrio - (nm) glass

viejo - (adj) old, aged; (nm) old man

viento - (nm) wind

vientre - (nm) abdomen; belly

viernes - (nm) Friday

violeta - (adj & nf) violet

visión - (nf) vision; sight

visita - (nf) visit, visitor

visitar - (vt) to visit; call on

vista - (nf) sight; vision

vitaminas - (nf) vitamin

vivienda - (nf) dwelling, house, abode

vivir - (vi & t) to live

vivo - (adj) alive, vivid, quick

volar - (vi & t) to fly

volcán - (nm) volcano

volver - (vi) to return

voz - (nf) voice; shout; clamor

vuelta - (nf) turn; walk

y

y - (nf) letter "y"; (conj) and

ya - (adv) already

yarda - (nf) yard (measure); yardstick

yerba - (nf) grass (Cuban)

yo - (pers pron) I, ego, self

Z

zacate - (nm) hay, grass

zanahoria - (nf) carrot

zapato - (nm) shoe

zeta - (nf) name of the letter "z"

zumbar - (vi) to buzz; to hum

Las Matemáticas

The following sections will prove useful in the development of lessons in mathematics. Basic numbers have already been taught (Section IV). Following are a guide for fractional number formation, as well as useful mathematical vocabulary.

I. Fractional numbers from 1/2 to 1/10 inclusive correspond more or less to the ordinal numbers:

un medio	1/2	*un sexto*	1/6
uno y medio	1 1/2	*un séptimo*	1/7
una y media	1 1/2	*un octavo*	1/8
		un ochavo	1/8
un tercio	1/3	*un noveno*	1/9
un cuarto	1/4	*un décimo*	1/10
un quinto	1/5		

II. From 1/11 onward, they are formed from the cardinals by adding the termination *avo*.

un onzavo or *once-avo*	1/11
un dozavo or *doce-avo*	1/12
un treintavo	1/30
un sesentavo	1/60
un centavo or *centésimo*	1/100
un milésimo	1/1000

III. The denominator assumes the plural form when the numerator is greater than one:

dos tercios	2/3	*cuatro quintos*	4/5
tres cuartos	3/4	*cinco octavos*	5/8

simple - single
doble or *duplicado* - double
triple or *triplicado* - triple
cuadruplo or *cuadruplicado* - quadruple
quintuplo or *quintuplicado* - fivefold
séxtuplo - sixfold (sexfold)
décuplo or *decuplado* - tenfold
céntuplo or *centuplicado* - a hundred fold

Las Matemáticas

a

Spanish to English	English to *Spanish*
ábaco – abacus	abacus – *ábaco*
abstracto – abstract	abstract – *abstracto*
abierto – open	add – *agregar, añadir, sumar*
acortar – to shorten	addend – *sumando*
adición – addition	addition – *suma, adición*
agregar – to add	algebra – *álgebra*
agrupar – to group	algorithm – *algoritmo*
alargar – to lengthen	analagous – *análogo*
álgebra – algebra	angle – *ángulo*
algoritmo – algorithm	area – *área*
altura – height, latitude	arrange – *ordenar*
análogo – analagous	ascending – *ascendente*
ancho – wide	
anchura – width	
ángulo – angle	
anterior – preceding	
añadir – to add	
área – area	
ascendente – ascending	

b

Spanish to <u>English</u>	<u>English</u> to *Spanish*
bajar - to reduce, to lower	balance - *balanza*
balanza - scale, balance	base - *base*
báscula - scale	belonging - *pertenencia*
base - base	

C

Spanish to English	English to Spanish
cambio - change	cardinal - cardinal
cantidad - quantity	carry out - ejecutar
caracterizar - to characterize	centigrade - centígrado
cardinal - cardinal	centimeter - centímetro
centígrado - centigrade	change - vuelta, cambio
centimetro - centimeter	characteristic - cualidad, característica
cero - zero	characterize - caracterizar
cerrado - closed	check - comprobar
cifra - number, cipher	cipher - cifra
círculo - circle	circle - círculo
circunferencia - circumference	circumference - circunferencia
clasificar - to classify	classify - clasificar
colección - collection	closed - cerrado
columnar - column	coin - moneda
comparar - to compare	collection - colección
compartimiento - compartment	compare - comparar
compás - compass	compartment - compartimiento
complemento - complement	complement - complemento
comprobar - to verify, check	complete - llenar
concreto - concrete	concrete - concreto
conjunción - conjunction	conjunction - conjunción
conjunto - set	contrary - contrario
contadores - counters	continuous - contínuo
contar - to count	convergent - convergente

Spanish to English	English to Spanish
contínuo - continuous	cube - *cubo*
contrario - opposite	
convergente - convergent	
corto - short	
correspondencia - correspondence	
cuadrado - square	
cualidad - quality, characteristic	
cuarto de galón - quart	
cuaterno - quaternary	
cubo - cube	
cuociente - quotient	

<u>*Spanish*</u> to <u>English</u>

chico - little

Spanish to English	English to *Spanish*
decena – a quantity of ten	decimal – *decimal*
decimal – decimal	decimeter – *decímetro*
decímetro – decimeter	deduction – *deducción*
deducción – deduction	degree – *grado*
derecha – right side	descending – *descendente*
derecho – straight	diagonal – *diagonal*
descendente – descending	diameter – *diámetro*
descubrimiento – discovery	difference – *diferencia, resta*
desigualdad – dissimilarity, inequality	different – *diferente*
diagonal – diagonal	digit – *dígito*
diámetro – diameter	dimension – *dimensión*
diferencia – difference	dimensional – *dimensional*
diferente – different	discontinuous – *discontinuo*
dígito – digit	discovery – *descubrimiento*
dimensión – dimension	disjunction – *disjunción*
dimensional – dimensional	dissimilarity – *desigualdad*
discontinuo – discontinuous	diverse – *diverso*
disjunción – disjunction	divided by – *dividido por*
diverso – diverse	division – *división*
dividido por – divided by	divisor – *divisor*
división – division	domain – *dominio*
divisor – divisor	domino – *dominó*
dominio – domain	
dominó – domino	

e

Spanish to _English_	_English_ to _Spanish_
ecuación - equation	empty - *vacío*
ejecutar - to carry out, to perform	encase - *encajar*
encajar - to encase	equal - *equal*
equivalencia - equivalency	equal (to be) - *equivaler*
equivalente - equivalent	equation - *ecuación*
equivaler - to be equal, equivalent	equivalency - *equivalencia*
escala - scale (measure)	equivalent - *equivalente*
esquema - outline, sketch, plan	extension - *extensión*
extensión - extension	

f

Spanish to <u>English</u>	<u>English</u> to *Spanish*
factor - factor	factor - *factor*
faltar - to be lacking	fill - *llenar*
forma - form, shape	form - *forma*
fórmula - formula	formula - *fórmula*
fracción - fraction	fraction - *fracción*
	full - *lleno*

Spanish to English	English to Spanish
galón - gallon	gallon - *galón*
geo - geo	geo - *geo*
geometría - geometry	geometry - *geometría*
geométrico - geometric	geometric - *geométrico*
goma - rubber band	graph - *gráfica*
grado - degree	greater - *major*
gráfica - graph	group - *agrupar*
gramo - gram	
grande - large	
grupo - group	

h

Spanish to English	English to *Spanish*
hexágono – hexagon	half – *medio, mitad*
hipotenusa – hypotenuse	height – *altura*
horizontal – horizontal	hexagon – *hexágono*
hueco – hollow	hollow – *hueco*
	horizontal – *horizontal*
	hypotenuse – *hipotenusa*

i

Spanish to English	English to *Spanish*
idéntico - identical	ice cream sticks - *palos de helados*
igual - equal	identical - *idéntico*
igual a - equal to	implication - *implicación*
impar - odd (number)	inch - *pulgada*
implicación - implication	inclusion - *inclusión*
inclusión - inclusion	inequality - *desigualdad*
inferencia - inference	inference - *inferencia*
intersección - intersection	intersection - *intersección*
inverso - inverse	inverse - *inverso*
irregular - irregular	irregular - *irregular*
izquierda - left side	

Spanish to <u>English</u>　　　　**ǀ**　　　<u>English</u> to *Spanish*

juntar - join　　　　　　　　join - *unir, juntar*

k

Spanish to English	English to Spanish
kilo - kilo	kilo - *kilo*
kilogramo - kilogram	kilogram - *kilogramo*
kilómetro - kilometer	kilometer - *kilómetro*

Spanish to English	English to Spanish
ley - rule norm	lack (to be) - *faltar*
línea - line	large - *grande*
línea numeral - number line	latitude - *altura*
litro - liter	least - *menor*
lógica - logic	left side - *izquierda*
longitud - length	length - *longitud*
	lengthen - *alargar*
	less - *menos*
	line - *línea*
	liter - *litro*
	logic - *lógica*
	longitude - *longitud*
	lower - *bajar*

Spanish to English

llenar - to fill, to complete

lleno - full

m

Spanish to English	English to Spanish
manipulación - handling, manipulation	manipulation - manipulación
más - plus; more	match - parear
matemáticas - math	mathematics - matemáticas
mayor - greater	measure - medir, medida
medida - measure, proportion	meter - metro
medio - half, middle	middle - medio
medir - to measure	millimeter - milímetro
menor - least	minuend - minuendo
menos - less	missing (to be) - faltar
metro - meter	model - patron
milímetro - millimeter	more - más
minuendo - minuend	multiplication - multiplicación
mitad - half	multiply - multiplicar
moneda - coin	
multiplicación - multiplication	
multiplicar - multiply	

_n_

Spanish to English	English to Spanish
negación - negation	negation - _negación_
nexo - bond, connection, nexus	nexus - _nexo_
numerar - to number, to count	norm - _ley_
número - number, numeral	number - _cifra, número, numerar_
número par - even number	number line - _línea numeral_
número impar - odd number	numerous - _numeroso_

Spanish to English	English to Spanish
objeto - object	object - *objeto*
operación - operation	odd - *impar*
orden - order	open - *abierto*
ordenar - to order, arrange	operation - *operación*
ordinal - ordinal	opposite - *contrario*
organizador - organizer	order - *order, ordenar*
	ordinal - *ordinal*
	organizer - *organizador*
	outline - *esquema*

P

Spanish to English	English to Spanish
palito - rod	pair (to) - *parear*
palos de helados - popsicle sticks	pairing - *pareo*
par - even	parallel - *paralelo*
paralelo - parallel	part - *parte*
parear - to pair, to match	pattern - *patrón*
pareo - pairing, coupling, matching	perform - *ejecutar*
parte - part	pentagon - *pentágono*
patrón - pattern, model	perimeter - *perímetro*
pentágono - pentagon	pi - *pi*
perímetro - perimeter	pint - *pinta*
pertenencia - belonging	plus - *más*
pesa - scale	polygon - *polígono*
pi - pi π	popsicle stick - *palos de helados*
pinta - pint	position - *rango*
polígono - polygon	preceding - *anterior*
progreso - progress	progress - *progreso*
propiedad - property	proof - *prueba*
prueba - proof	property - *propiedad*
pulgada - inch	proportion - *medida*
	protractor - *transportador*

Spanish to English	English to *Spanish*
quitar - to remove, to be away	quality - *cualidad*
	quantity of ten - *decena*
	quart - *cuarto de galón*
	quaternary - *cuaterno*
	quotient - *cuociente*

Spanish to English	English to Spanish
radio - radius	radius - *radio*
rango - range	range - *rango*
razón - ratio	ratio - *razón*
reagrupación - regroup	reciprocal - *recíproca*
recíproca - reciprocal	rectangle - *rectángulo*
rectángulo - rectangle	recurrence - *recurrencia*
recto - straight	regroup - *reagrupar*
recurrencia - recurrence	regular - *regular*
redondo - round	remainder - *resta*
regla - ruler	remove - *quitar*
regular - regular	resolution - *resolución*
resolución - resolution	result - *resultado*
resolver - to resolve	reunion - *reunión*
resta - difference; remainder	right side - *derecha*
restar - to subtract	rod - *palito, vara*
resultado - result	round - *redondo*
	rubber band - *goma*
	ruler - *regla*

Spanish to English	English to Spanish
sección - segment	scale - escala (metric) pesa (weight)
segmento - segment	segment - sección, segmento
semejante - similar	separate - separar
separar - separate	series - serie
serie - series	set - conjunto
signo - sign, symbol	shape - forma
simetría - symmetry	short - corto
subordinado - sub	shorten - acortar
substracción - subtraction	sign - signo, símbolo
substraendo - subtrahend	similar - semejante
suma - sum	size - tamaño
sumando - addend	sketch - esquema
sumar - to add	skill - destreza
	solve - resolver
	square - cuadrado
	straight - derecho, recto
	sub - subordinado
	subtract - restar
	subtraction - substracción, resta (n)
	subtrahend - substraendo
	sum - suma
	symmetry - simetría

Spanish to English	English to Spanish
tabla (de multiplicar) - multiplication table	table - *tabla*
tamaño - size	take away - *quitar*
temperatura - temperature	temperature - *temperatura*
termómetro - thermometer	ten (quantity of) - *decena*
transformación - transformation	thermometer - *termómetro*
triángulo - triangle	transformation - *transformación*
	triangle - *triángulo*

u

Spanish to English	English to Spanish
unidad - unity, unit	unit - *unidad*
unir - to unite, to join	unity - *unidad*

V

Spanish to English	English to Spanish
valor - value	value - *valor*
valer - to be worth	verify - *comprobar*
vara - rod	vertical - *vertical*
vecindad - vicinity	vicinity - *vecindad*
vertical - vertical	volume - *volumen*
volumen - volume	
vuelta - reverse, change (money)	

W

<u>*Spanish*</u> to <u>English</u>

<u>English</u> to <u>*Spanish*</u>

width - *anchura*

wide - *ancho*

worth (to be) - *valer (v)*
              valor (n)

Spanish to English	English to Spanish
zero - zero	zero - zero, cero